YOUR SPIRITUAL IQ

JOHN S. SAVAGE

YOUR SPIRITUAL IQ

Five Steps to Spiritual Growth

ABINGDON PRESS
Nashville

YOUR SPIRITUAL IQ
FIVE STEPS TO SPIRITUAL GROWTH

This book is printed on acid-free paper.

Library of Congress Cataloging-in-Publication Data

Savage, John S.
Your spiritual IQ : five steps to spiritual growth / John S. Savage.
p. cm.
Includes bibliographical references.
ISBN 978-1-4267-0219-8 (pbk. : alk. paper)
1. Spiritual formation. I. Title.
BV4511.S37 2010
248—dc22

2009025850

10 11 12 13 14 15 16 17 18 19—10 9 8 7 6 5 4 3 2 1

MANUFACTURED IN THE UNITED STATES OF AMERICA

To my wife, Joyce, with whom

I can dialogue about deeply spiritual things

Contents

Foreword ix

Step I: Know Your Own Story: Be a Witness 1

Step II: Pray Deeply: Dialogue with God 27

Step III: Simplify Your Desires: Learn to Meditate, Reflect, and Contemplate 49

Step IV: Face Your Challenges: Finding God in the Spiritual Desert Times 81

Step V: Expand Your Understanding: Learn, Find Meaning in Your Life, and Be in Mission for Others 91

A Brief Summary 127

Appendix: Tools to Develop a Personal Spiritual Development Plan 129

Notes 141

Bibliography 143

Foreword

Jan, a fifty-year-old woman, sat across the table from me. We were in a restaurant and had a private booth with no one nearby. What I heard from her started my quest to try and understand how she became such a congruent, intelligent Christian. I have listened to hundreds of persons in my life—after all, that is both my passion and my calling. But something special happened in listening to Jan that I had not been aware of before.

She was able to articulate what she believed about God and Christ in such a profound way that if I had not already been a believer, I would certainly have considered becoming one. She was soft in her approach and personal in her demeanor. I was aware that she was in touch with the deep feelings that were within her because her tone of voice and the occasional tears in her eyes said just as much as any word she uttered. She was congruent and authentic. She could articulate her experiences both with God and with others. It was as if God were her closest friend and that her relationship was renewed daily.

When I asked her questions about how that relationship had developed, she told me story after story of how using prayer was essential in developing rapport with God. Her way of using prayer had started in her early childhood, but had mostly developed after midlife, particularly after a series of life events that caused her to doubt what she had been taught in her church. That shifting of faith time, a time I call desert time, came about as a result of an intense struggle about the nature of God. Jan began to alter some of her beliefs about God. Most of all, she changed how she saw herself and how she thought about herself. I would like to add that this shift of faith did not motivate her to move to another church. She has stayed faithful to her current church because it allows a variety of beliefs about God within its system.

These changes that occurred deep inside her manifested themselves in many ways. She changed her career from that of a business executive to a full-time teacher in a Christian organization. This offered her deep meaning, both because she could influence persons more directly about their faith and because she had the opportunity to return to school to get an advanced degree.

The above comments led me to another awareness of the intelligent Christian. Jan never stopped learning. Jan was the epitome of the person who was forever on the move to learn about the world, others, herself, and how God was in it all.

I took notes as fast I could so I could gather the essence of what I was hearing. Then another characteristic came to my attention that I should have already known but did not. The intelligent Christian has an identified life mission and can readily talk about it. Jan's mission was clear as a bell. She wanted to teach, but most of all she wanted to help people find the best relationship possible with God.

In the midst of this interview, a rather subtle and understated concept emerged as an important element in Jan's spiritual intelligence. Each of the experiences that she shared was laced with concepts of meaning. Phrases such as "this meant to me" or "I had to find in the experience its deeper meaning" became consistent throughout our conversation. Consequently, bringing meaning to life's events became one of the significant characteristics of Jan's spiritual intelligence.

As a result of interviewing this dedicated person and many others like her, I have found a set of useful and consistent factors in the highly developed spiritually intelligent person. Thus, this book is a reflection of two primary areas: first, the exploration of those findings; and second, how an individual or group of individuals can develop these characteristics.

Though Jan was one of the first persons I interviewed, what I learned from her and the others gave me the insight to write about what I learned. This book is the result of the expression of these persons of deep faith who live congruently, make statements of their faith, live their lives in the act of unending learning, and who have had to struggle with the meaning of life and all that it offers. In all of that spiritual developing, these persons have grown to become the kinds of people who are living out their Christian lives in the community, working on changing that community, and serving God in the many different aspects of her life.

This book would not have been possible without the help of the persons in a variety of religious systems who allowed me to interview them. They include persons who belong to the following churches: United Methodist, Roman Catholic, Anglican, Christian Church (Disciples of Christ), Presbyterian, Southern Baptist, American Baptist, Evangelical Lutheran Church of America, Nazarene, Salvation Army, Quaker, The Uniting Church of Australia, and The United Church of Canada. I am deeply grateful to them all.

A Spiritual Jolt

About two years before this book was published I took part in a prayer vigil in a church that has a beautiful stained-glass window at the front of the worship area. There was a kneeler placed in front of the altar (Communion Table). The sanctuary had been dimmed to enhance the silence. I moved and knelt on the prayer bench and focused on the well-lighted stained-glass window of Jesus kneeling in the garden of Gethsemane. In a moment of meditation I imagined myself kneeling next to Jesus. I asked, "Jesus, do you have a word for me?" The response was startling, fast, and clear. "Write," he said. This book is a response to that command.

An Overview

What I heard from the persons I interviewed was remarkable. Regardless of their denomination or faith orientation, I found the same qualities repeating themselves over and over. At first I thought it might be the questions I asked, but then I noticed that my questions were quite open-ended, allowing the respondents to go wherever they wanted in their answers. For example: "What have been your most significant religious experiences, and when did they take place?" Or "What has most guided or influenced you to become the kind of Christian you are today?" Because my interview style is to follow the agenda of the interviewee, I followed up their answers with more questions to get more in-depth information and insights.

I have divided this book into a foreword, five chapters, a brief summary, and a Personal Spiritual Development Plan, and notes with a select bibliography.

Here is an overview of this book.

Step I. Know your own story. This step covers the first of five predictable characteristics of the spiritually intelligent person. Another way of stating this is that such a person has the ability to be a witness to his or her own religious experience. Though "knowing your own story" is much more complex than this one statement, it is a key factor. After all, if persons do not have this skill, they would not be able to pass their faith to the next generation.

Step II. Pray deeply. The second characteristic is the skill of prayer. Each spiritually intelligent person has a profound prayer life. This step explores what that means and also introduces a variety of forms of prayer that can be used in the development of praying persons' relationship with God. It explores in detail how we communicate with God and also how God communicates with us.

Step III. Simplify your desires. In this step I will present what I learned from these persons' ability to meditate, reflect, and contemplate. This section introduces the important skills of silence and how to be still. A series of strategies will be presented to help the reader develop these spiritual characteristics.

Step IV. Face your challenges. The fourth spiritual intelligence is the willingness to be stripped down inside so that internal struggles are used to build character and understanding; or, in brief, it is the experience of entering spiritual desert time. This section of the book is devoted to understanding what happens when faith goes through major changes. Each of the persons I interviewed had these intense spiritual experiences, and they were able to use the desert times to discover and they greatly benefited from the intense relationship with God that occurred. Most people became very frightened of this stage of spiritual development and simply tried to avoid it. It is my intent to share in depth the things that are necessary to go through the desert time with meaningful persistence and purpose.

Step V. Expand your understanding. Within a very few minutes of the start of the interviews, the fifth of these characteristics became very obvious to me. In fact, most of the people started by telling me something that fell into this category. In its shortened version it is the ability to be in mission for others: "To share one's self with the world both in and beyond the local church." Another way of stating this: "To discover and act on your deepest passion for living." This chapter will give you strategies and processes to identify your deepest drives and emotions so that you may be able to act on them and thus find the deepest meaning for yourself by giving yourself to others.

Giving yourself to others could not develop were it not for the ability to study and learn throughout your lifetime for the purpose of expanding knowledge and understanding of yourself and others. Regardless of their theology, these persons were committed to ongoing education and training in their lives, so this chapter will be devoted to identifying many ways these persons continued to grow personally and in their faith. Without this growing edge these persons would have "dried up" and would have not been able to stay alert, active, and healthy.

The combination of these characteristics led to a deep and important concept: the ability to find meaning in all things and events of life. It became for these people the process of discovering meaning and purpose in all that they did. It shows up in their ability to be at peace with themselves. It is the process of becoming consistent in living out the Christian faith. It is this characteristic that allowed these people to discover deeper meaning and purpose, both in the pain and the joy of their lives. Regardless of what happened to them, they were able to find God's/Christ's presence in their midst.

A Brief Summary. The final chapter of this book tells how you can put these five steps into practice in your own life and in that of your faith community. We will also explore a Personal Spiritual Development Plan (PSDP).

It is my hope that this book will provide a very significant resource to help you work on your own spiritual intelligence and devote yourself to expanding and mastering the five spiritual intelligences. Find persons within your own faith communities and urge them to join you in this journey of spiritual intelligence. You may find it to be one of the most rewarding things you have ever done in your religious journey.

STEP I

Know Your Own Story: Be a Witness

If one advances confidently in the direction of his dreams, and endeavors to live the life which he has imagined, he will meet with a success unexpected in common hours.

—*Henry David Thoreau*

To begin a spiritual journey requires strong intent, so I encourage those of you who want to begin to say, "I am loved by God, and there is nothing I can do to stop it." But in order to say that with conviction, it is important to know who you are as a person, and particularly who you are as a Christian person. So the first step begins by knowing yourself as intimately as possible.

Gloria came to see me as a referral from her physician. It is unusual for me to have a doctor refer a patient to me, but it did happen. The only detail you really need to know concerns one aspect of her spiritual journey. She had found Christ in a powerful personal experience, but her relationship with Christ was not a healthy one. For example, every morning she asked Jesus what clothes she should put on and what to have for breakfast. Sadly, she could not make any decision without being told what to do by Christ, or by anyone else for that matter.

In one of our sessions I leaned forward and moved within two feet of her, looked directly at her, and asked in a soft voice, "Who are you in there?" She answered with a whisper, "I am nothing." Then with increasing repetitions of the statement she said, "I am nothing, I am nothing, I am nothing," until the statement turned into a scream: "*I . . . am . . . nothing!*"

The key search of the Christian is to find out who he or she is for God's sake. Jesus' statements "I am the good shepherd" or "I am the light of the world" are characteristics of his identity and mission. He knew who he was and what his life was about.

This is the first step toward increased spiritual intelligence. The spiritually intelligent Christian has the ability to state what he or she believes about God, others, and self, including the ability to share with another the experience of one's own personal journey and its meaning.

So let us begin our journey. I ask you to explore your own understanding of what constitutes a spiritually intelligent person. Pause for a moment and let your mind think of a person in your church, family, or work whom you would identify as someone who has matured as a Christian. Make sure that you look across the age span. There are sixteen-year-old mature Christians and eighty-year-old immature Christians. What characteristics help you draw that conclusion?

In listening to the persons I interviewed, there was one characteristic that quickly became obvious. All of them had a wonderful story of their faith in God and could clearly articulate it to me. They were not ashamed of sharing with me or with others. This one competency is important. Here is why.

We are now one hundred generations away from when Christ was personally on our planet, given that each generation is about twenty years. Imagine, if you can, where your great-grandparents (100 times over) lived on this earth. Where did they live when

Jesus was here? You did have relatives who were alive when Jesus lived his thirty-three years on earth. Now consider this: someone told someone at least one hundred times, once in each generation, about Jesus and God's love, or you would have never heard the good news of God's love. So it is imperative that we learn the skills of sharing our Christian faith with others.

Behaviors You Need to Skillfully Share Your Faith

I want you to be able to use each of the skills that will be presented in this book on a daily basis. Your faith story may be a simple statement of your own experience. Think about your story, and when you hear those of other persons, compliment them.

Recently, my wife and I were in a restaurant for lunch. At a table next to our booth were three women and two small children; I guess the children were about two years old. The children were well behaved, ate what was given to them, and paid attention to the adults. Two of the women were the mothers of the two children. I complimented them as I left, saying I appreciated how well behaved the kids had been. They smiled as if I had made their day. Sharing good news brings hope and help to those who receive it. Try it. Bring hope in every setting you can.

In order to act in affirming ways to another person, you have to become aware of your own self-affirmation—that is, how do you affirm yourself?

The next section of this chapter will give you some tools to use in recognizing that you are a person of worth in the heart of God, which will enable you to share that experience with others by both what you say and what you do.

Direct Expression of Feelings

Sharing your personal experience with another person requires that you are congruent. Congruency is the ability to give the same message with your words, tone of voice, and body language. To authentically share with another, these three things must be aligned with one another.

I sat with a woman in a spiritual direction session. She was sharing with me how God had helped her with a series of problems that were life threatening to her and her family. While telling me this story, which would have scared anyone who experienced it, she sat with a big, fixed grin on her face. The behavior was incongruent with the story she told me. I learned over the many sessions I spent with her that when she was a child she was not permitted to cry or show any sad emotion, so she created this smile to survive in the family setting. She was not allowed to directly express her emotions. They were suppressed. Now, when she goes to share her faith and personal experience with another person, her body tells one story and her words tell another. The result is that people are not quite sure what to believe. Do they believe the message of what her story is telling or the body language that accompanies it? My experience is that we believe a person from the body up. Namely, the body rarely lies because it is operated by the unconscious. Trust the body language and compare that with the rest of the message.

There is a powerful message in Dr. Patricia Cook's doctoral dissertation that illustrates both the use of religious language and how she learned to share her faith. Please be aware of the amount of religious language.

> Within the first couple weeks [of Dr. Cook's ministry at her church], Patricia [referring to herself] began a preaching series entitled "What are we selling?" Not highly theological, this

> seemed to engage the congregation as an appropriate summer series, especially for a new pastor. The congregation heard the message, "If we're not selling Jesus, I'm in the wrong church." The church's key lay leader told Patricia early on that the congregation was buzzing about how much she had preached about Jesus, remarking that no pastor in fifty years had done so.
>
> She remembered how hungry for Jesus she used to be. Growing up in Kettering, Ohio, she attended confirmation classes where she learned the catechism of the Presbyterian Church, memorizing the Apostle's Creed, learning about the structure of the church and its theology. But no one ever said, "I believe in Jesus and here's why . . ." It all seemed so impersonal, that by the time she got to high school during the end of the sixties, she and her high school sweetheart agreed that neither of them had a clue who Jesus was even though they had both grown up in the church. Both of them agreed that they believed in God, but that Jesus was irrelevant.
>
> It wasn't until her grandfather died toward the end of her time in college that she and her mother flew to Miami, Florida, where she met an estranged aunt who was in love with Jesus. She accepted all of Patricia's questions on the subject and began to send her books by C. S. Lewis and Corrie Ten Boom. But it was the fact that she seemed to be made of love that drew Patricia to her. She also gave Patricia a Living Bible. Starting in the New Testament, she read about people who were in love with Jesus, and by the time she got to John's gospel and the post-resurrection story where the disciples are in the boat fishing in despair, she had fallen in love with Jesus, too. . . . Becoming an avid volunteer in her in-laws' church, she even gave a testimony from the pulpit one Sunday. After that, she was never afraid to tell anyone about Jesus.[1]

Dr. Cook learned how to risk and share her faith. Knowing her as I do, I can testify that she is in touch with her emotions and she uses them appropriately. So how does a person get in touch with his or her emotional life? How do we learn to use and develop kinesthetic language—verbal language that expresses and names specific emotions—to help express our faith?

In guiding persons to become more awake to their emotions, there are several approaches.

1. Ask them to remember a specific event that produced fairly strong emotions.
2. Ask them to become aware of any physical response to that event, and to experience it as intensely as they can. They may be aware of it as tension in the stomach, back, upper chest, neck, or any part of the body where the person holds tension.
3. Ask them if that part of their body could talk, what would it say? Let it tell them what it is experiencing. Most likely it will give a story of the experience or name an emotion. Words that come out might be *sad*, *angry*, *fearful*, or *hurt*. It may be a positive memory of joy, happiness, loving-kindness, or peacefulness, and so forth.

The following is an example of a person with great difficulty in expressing emotions. A woman called and made an appointment to see me, but she did not say why she wanted to come. After her arrival, she sat down in her chair and remained quiet. I asked her what had brought her to see me. She remained quiet. I sat back in my chair and waited. We sat quietly for several minutes with neither of us speaking. I asked her if it was difficult to talk to me about the problem. She nodded her head yes. I asked her if she could just make a sound of any kind. Out came a very weak sound like that of a little child beginning to groan—a kind of an "aaaauuuuuggggh." I asked her to let it get louder. She did so slightly. I encouraged her to bring it out more, and she did but only slightly. She put her head into her hands. I asked if she could let the sound become a word, any word, and very softly but clearly she said, "help," and then in consecutive breaths she said the word over and over but each time with more volume until it was a full-blown scream. Then the emotions broke through and she began to cry profusely. She was now in touch with the emotion. She cried for a few minutes and then was able to tell me about the events that had occurred, and we were finally able to talk about them.

All of us struggle, to some degree, to be consciously in touch with our emotions. Daniel Goleman says: "Self-awareness—recognizing a feeling *as it happens*—is the keystone of emotional intelligence . . . the ability to monitor feelings from moment to moment is crucial to psychological insight and self-understanding. An inability to notice our true feelings leaves us at their mercy. People with great certainty about their feelings are better pilots of their lives, having a sense of how they really feel about personal decisions from whom to marry to what job to take."[2]

I have come to believe that it is very difficult to be spiritually intelligent if you are emotionally stupid. As we will see later in this book, God uses our emotions as one of the key ways in which God communicates with us. It is important to develop emotional intelligence so that you can become a sensitive witness of God's love to another.

Give people permission to feel and to learn the language of how to express their feelings. When you share your story with another, please pay attention to two things that go on simultaneously. Be aware of what you are feeling as you share your story and pay attention to the response you get from the person when you are listening. This fosters your ability to build rapport and trust, allowing you to be more congruent so that the person with whom you are sharing will move emotionally toward you and not away from you, encouraging the person to be more open to what you have to say.

Early in my pastoral ministry I was an aggressive witness of my faith and as one person put it, "I backed people into a corner until they cried *Jesus.*" I am not that way anymore. Why? It did not work. In those days it was more important for me to share what I wanted to say than to pay attention to other people's questions and what they had to say. Please be a listener first before you share your own journey and witness. After all, if you are talking about the love of God, but not showing that love in word, tone, and body language, you have become incongruent and the other person will not trust your message.

There is a phrase I have come to trust: "The response you get is the message you sent." So always be aware of the response you are getting from the other person. If you are getting something you do not feel is appropriate, ask yourself, "What am I doing to get that response?" It may be that you will need to change your own behavior in order to get a different reaction. Pay as much attention to your own behavior as to that of the person with whom you are sharing your witness of faith.

An Exercise in Emotional Awareness

There are many places and times when you can practice this wonderful skill. The next time you are with someone, simply pay attention to what is going on inside of you while you are in that person's presence. Are you comfortable with the person or do you sense some anxiety or anger? The response in you is often what is in them. Learn to trust your tummy.

On one of my trips to Australia, I was told a wonderful story about such awareness. Icky, the main character in this story, is asked to train a group of young boys how to listen. He says, "Boys, I want to give you your first lesson in listening. I want you to learn how to listen with your tummy." One of the little boys says, "Is me belly button me ear?" "Yes," says Icky. "Your belly button is your ear. Learn to listen with your tummy, smell with your eyes, and see with your ears." It is using this sensitivity with others that will build the kind of relationship that will allow the listener to receive your message.

Harold Wooten, who is a friend, colleague, and author, has produced a marvelous training event called "Powerful Presentations—It's All about an Authentic You!" He teaches that the student should learn to be transparent; that is, without pretense or deception. It is that kind of behavior and attitude that leads to the best kind of witness.

It became apparent to me that the persons I interviewed were such genuine, authentic Christians that it would have been difficult not to accept their witness.

Understanding Your Beliefs

In sharing your story and your beliefs about God or Christ it might be helpful for you to understand how beliefs are formed, not only in you but also in the person with whom you are sharing. In my book *Listening and Caring Skills*,[3] I share in depth how we get our belief system, but here is the core of that material: the concepts of belief development are crucial to understanding how a belief is formed and how best to share your beliefs with another person.

Developing Kinesthetic Beliefs: I Believe What I Feel

Your belief systems, those beliefs that make up your understanding of the world, are shaped from your earliest childhood.

During the first three years of life the brain is growing at the rate of one to three million synaptic connections per second. We are in fact getting wired for life. During this time, the brain does not just learn from words but from tone of voice, visual clues (like the smile of the mother), and from emotional experiences (how the world feels). When the children have a secure setting, they are able to be open to both the love and caring of others. They will respond appropriately. By far, the first years of life are the most important because children base their beliefs not just on oral teachings but from the experiences they are having. These years are what I call the kinesthetic years—the years of the initial development of emotions. To put it succinctly, "I believe what I feel." These feelings often act as commandments for our behavior later on in life, thus I use the language of "Life Commandments." This level of growth is crucial to spiritual development because God communicates through our experiences (see Step II). Those feelings of early childhood reside with us most of our lives. They can enhance our potential or they can limit it.

In my spiritual direction work with individuals, I notice that frequently they experience fear in coming close to God. An intimate relation seems out of the question and often intimidating to the person. When exploring that resistance I find that there is a strong belief based on the person's kinesthetic experience that "if you get too close, you will get hurt." Sometimes this can become extreme and a profound dilemma in the person's life.

I worked with a woman who told me that in her early years (three to four years old) her father would ask her to come and sit on his lap. When she did, he would slap her hands and tell her to never trust a man. She would back up from him, crying, and then her father would say, "Your father loves you. Come and give him a hug." As she moved toward him, in the hopes of getting some comfort by giving him a hug, he again would slap her hands and say, "Never trust a man." As the little girl again moved away he would say, "Come here. Don't you love your father?" Such early experiences create deep emotional internal conflict. When you move close, you get hurt; when you move away, you feel guilty.

I share this story because there are times when you share your experience of God or Christ and the other person's response may be that he or she does not believe in God at all, because "no good God would ever do bad things to his children." Convincing them otherwise will be a difficult job.

Verbal Life Commandments

A second set of beliefs develops from commands from those around us. These produce what I call *Verbal Life Commandments*. These statements may be spoken only once or they may be repeated hundreds of times. These commandments often become the guiding force in our lives. Recently, I sat with a man who kept repeating the phrases, "But my mother said . . ." ". . . my father said . . ." He was fifty-eight years old and still running his life by the commands of his parents. In middle childhood the brain is relatively nondifferentiated. That is, it cannot tell the difference between one truth and another. If one adult tells you that you are stupid, dumb, and will never amount to anything, whereas another says that you are the smartest kid in the class, that you are a gift from God, and very special, your brain has the ability to accept both at the same time. Later in life, those early beliefs take on theological significance and language, that is, I am saint and sinner, or as a Roman Catholic nun in Toronto said, "We are all gifted and all flawed."

You, the witness, need to be aware of both your own beliefs that have been formed by verbal commands from others and those that you share with another person. This step is an attempt to get you in touch with your deepest beliefs about yourself and others in order to be a congruent messenger of God's love. Always be careful not to use polar theological language that can contribute to the person's "war with one's self."

Beliefs through Self-talk

Verbal commands only receive their power when you say them to yourself. For example, if I say to you, "You are smart and enjoyable to be around," but you say to yourself, "If you knew me you would never say that," what I said never made it into you. It isn't what someone else says to you that makes it into your belief system; it is only when you say it to yourself.

A woman in a training event in Vancouver said that when she was a young girl her father said to her, "You're the dumbest kid on the planet," but when he said that, she said to herself, "You're wrong, I'm smart." It is what she said to herself that made it into her world, and she rejected that which was different.

Another way of perceiving this is to recognize that the belief system is a large neuro-sort. The brain can only receive so much information at one time or it will become overwhelmed and seize up. So it does one of three things (the sorting process) with incoming information: accepts it as a truth, distorts it enough to change it so it is acceptable, or deletes it.

When you are sharing your beliefs with another, the person listening processes what you say in those three ways. What you usually do not know is what she just did with what you said. If you say that God loves her, but she says to herself, "God doesn't love me; nobody would ever want to love me," then what you said is deleted from her beliefs. However, if the person is beginning to question her own beliefs and is ready to consider another way of thinking about God/Christ and herself, then she is more likely to begin some new self-talk that can change her personal relationship with God/Christ—and that, of course, is what conversion is about.

The Power of Modeling

Another way we develop our beliefs is through modeling. Modeling is observing the behaviors of others—and doing what they would do because we want to be like them, or to be more likely to be liked by them. The frontal cortex of our brain is often referred to as our third eye. We see it represented in myths of giants who have one eye in the center of their foreheads. This network of cells learns by seeing; it is highly influenced by observation and models what it sees.

I remember a story one of my doctorate professors told, in which a few newborn kittens were placed in a box with vertical white and black lines. Other kittens were placed in a box with black and white horizontal line sinside. Each group was placed in the box before their eyes were opened and kept there until they had grown enough to see and move around on their own. When they were fed, they were blindfolded so that the only thing they ever saw were the black and white lines. When old enough to see and walk on their own, they were freed into a room with wooden chairs. The kittens that grew up only seeing vertical lines ran into the horizontal bars of the chair because they could not see them. The other kittens raised in the horizontal-lined box ran into the legs of the chair. Their brains had only developed what they saw. We become what we see.

Our world is made up of the hundreds of models that we have experienced in our lives. The more narrow our experiences, the less we see of the world. We then begin to believe that what we have seen is all there is. When we believe that, we begin to delete other possible ways of seeing the world. If we see our parents fighting all the time, then we begin to model that because, after all, what other ways are there for people to behave?

After we grow up enough, go to school, meet other adults, and sit with our friends and their families, our brains can observe other models. We learn about options. However, the model that is the most dominant, most repeated, is the one that often guides us the most.

I became intensely aware of this during my psychotherapy internship at Rochester General Hospital, in Rochester, New York. I walked into the hospital reception area to meet my first child patient who stood hand-in-hand with her mother. She was a beautiful seven-year-old child. I knelt to greet her; she smiled; we talked; and I told her that we were going to a wonderful playroom with lots of toys and things to do. She let go of her mother's hand and took mine, and we walked down the hallway to the therapy room.

As we walked into the room I noticed that her arms and face were covered with scratches. Her mother had told the intake therapist that the little girl hid in the closet, cutting herself with coat hangers; and I had been told this before I met her. Our time together was wonderful; she was verbal, quite creative in making things and drawing. In the weeks that followed, she stopped the self-mutilating behavior and her mother was pleased with the progress. After three months of meeting with her, she finished her time with me. We had a cure, right? Wrong. As long as she was coming to the hospital, her behavior changed. However, when that stopped, she returned home full-time to the cruelty of her father, who was a drug addict and who modeled very dysfunctional behavior. The daughter saw the many marks on her father's arms and she modeled them. Why? Because she wanted her father to like her and treat her kindly.

One final illustration that lets you know how much the model of caring can influence an outcome is in Joseph Chilton Pearce's book *The Death of Religion and the Rebirth of Spirit*. He tells this wonderful story:

> Years ago, a research group had some rabbits that were being used to test various drugs and vaccines. These animals were inoculated with viruses to see which pharmaceutical wonder might keep them alive the longest. The victims were kept in separate cages and all proceedings were carefully followed and noted in the records. One particular rabbit remained miraculously healthy throughout testing; fat and fit, its coat glowing regardless of the deadly viruses pumped into it—indeed, in its case every drug seemed a wonder drug. The mystery was finally resolved: The night caretaker of the animals had taken a fancy to this fortunate little creature, and rather than just feeding it, he took it out of the cage each evening and hugged, petted, and played with it. DNA is acutely sensitive to signals from its environment, particularly those molecules of emotion. The emotional centers that control the immune system are extremely sensitive to those molecules broadcast from every direction.[4]

Modeling is very powerful. Be and do what you want your children to be and do. As strong as the kinesthetic beliefs become, they are affected strongly by the process of self-talk.

What can you take from this and practice at home and everywhere you go? Model the behavior that you want from others. If you want kindness, model kindness; if you want forgiveness, then forgive. If you want patience, then be patient. Be what you want and there is a good chance it will come back to you. Jesus was the greatest modeler of all time.

Traumatic Life Experiences: I Believe What I Say to Myself When I Am Upset

The life-shaping beliefs we have explored often take years to develop because their impact requires that they be repeated and reinforced over and over again. But traumatic life experiences and their accompanying beliefs are frequently created in a split second. These can be wonderfully positive and life-giving or they can reduce your potential for a lifetime. I remember a story told by Ron Willingham in his book *When Good Isn't Good Enough*. This story tells of an event from Willingham's childhood that produced a belief that was as alive the day it was formed as it was the day he wrote about it. The story is very powerful. I have used it many times in my workshops.

As young boy, he loved making airplanes. He was proud of what he had accomplished and took it to show his father. He knew that his father would praise his work and was full of hope and anticipation. But when he held it out for his father to see, his father said, "Do you reckon he'll ever learn to make one *right*?" He was stunned by the comment, left the house, and went to the back alley where he crushed the plane into a garbage can. What was left in the boy was a belief that he could never make an airplane, and he never tried again. As Willingham explained:

> I remember standing there, my emotional equilibrium destroyed. . . . I crumbled up the airplane and threw it into the barrel. After doing this, I eased the lid back on the barrel and walked away—as defeated as anyone could ever be defeated.
>
> And here's the point of the story. Until this very day, over forty years later, I've never again attempted to make a model airplane. I never even considered it. It wasn't because I didn't

> want to make one. As I mentioned, airplanes were our greatest interest, and I desperately wanted one.
>
> My point is that this experience *convinced* me that I *couldn't* do it. And it was as if I had no hands, no mind, no coordination, no desire—no nothing—I was just as bound! It had nothing to do with my actual abilities. It was all due to my negative beliefs.[5]

Be careful what you say to yourself when you have a very sad experience. It just may last for a lifetime.

This formation of the brain remembering a strong emotional event was so powerful that years later, as an adult, he still obeyed it completely. Self-talk that you internalize when you are very upset can become a power memory and driver of behavior for many years, or until something replaces it. This includes our own religious experiences. In fact, many religious experiences are created through this process. An event of great emotional intensity can shape a person's faith and belief about God for a long time.

For many years, evangelists used highly emotional worship services to extract feelings of guilt and shame from the members of their congregations. These feelings often propelled people forward during the altar call. For many, this initial event is talked about years later as the "night I came to the Lord." For others, those same services became so negative that when they walked away from the service they said to themselves—while very upset—"I'm never going to go back to that place [church] again." And so it got anchored emotionally in a negative way and they never did go back. When you witness to another person, your mere presence and language may refire such events and you must try to understand the reaction and not be too quick to judge it. So be very careful what you say to yourself when you are emotionally distraught, because that self-talk just may become your reality.

Surprisingly, all life events are what you say to yourself they are. They become what you bring to them. The power of self-talk and your ability to transform the event into something that is incredibly life enhancing can be truly lifesaving.

Dr. Frankl, in his book *The Doctor and the Soul*, asks the following questions:

> Does not all this support the view that a character type is marked out by the environment? . . . Our answer is: it does not. But if not, where does man's inner freedom remain? Consider his behavior—is he still spiritually responsible for what is happening to him psychically, for what the concentration camp has "made" of him? Our answer is: he is. For even in the socially limited environment, in spite of this societal restriction upon his personal freedom, the ultimate freedom still remains his: the freedom even in the camp to give some shape to his existence. There are plenty of examples . . . to prove that even in the camps men could still "do differently" that they did not have to submit to the apparently almighty concentration-camp law of psychic deformation. In fact, the weight of evidence tends to show that the men who typified the character traits of the camp inmates, who had succumbed to the character-forming forces of the social environment, were those who had beforehand given up the struggle spiritually. The freedom to take what attitude they would toward the concrete situation had not been wrested from them; they had themselves withdrawn their claim to use that freedom. For whatever may have been taken from them in their first hour in camp . . . no one can wrest from a man his freedom to take one or another attitude toward his destiny. And alternative attitudes really did exist. Probably in every concentration camp there were individuals able to overcome their apathy and suppress their irritability . . . examples of renunciation and self-sacrifice. Asking nothing for themselves, they went about the grounds and in the barracks of the camp, offering a kind word here, a last crust of bread there.[6]

Frankl's illustration tells of the power of the culture in which we live. It forces us to consider Jesus' statement to "be in but not of this world."

I Believe What My Culture Tells Me

The life commandments or belief systems above come from specifically observed or experienced events. The cultural ones are more general in character, but still have incredible power. These cultural beliefs are the result of what a group, community, and country have come to believe about who they are, and what they are to do. They provide the context in which we live, because we simply take the beliefs for granted.

I have journeyed many times to Australia and have come to love and respect the Australian people and their culture. Like all countries, there are beliefs that are taught to their children from an early age. One particular belief sets limits on excellence for the individual. It is stated in the brief phrase "Cut down the tall poppy." The meaning of this phrase is "Do not aspire to be better than anyone else." If you begin to rise to the top of your class in school, you may be put down for your excellence.

I have been to Newfoundland six times. The Newfoundlanders I met, though they are now beginning to change their beliefs, told me that they are the "armpit of Canada." I am glad to report that I was there recently and found that belief was changing; in fact, they are increasingly proud of the resources they produce for the world, such as coal, oil, and timber.

We in the United States have many cultural life commandments. In fact, wherever I go, if I start a life commandment statement, most people can finish it for me. For example, if we are sitting at a dinner table and I say to you, "Finish this statement: 'Eat everything . . .' I bet you can finish it with 'on your plate.'" If I say, "Waste not . . . ," you'll add "want not." And if I say, "A penny saved is . . . ," you'll add "a penny earned." You can probably name many more.

Within our own churches we find many cultural rules that guide the congregation's behavior. Below is a series of beliefs that lead to a dysfunctional and highly limited life. If you believe these statements, what kind of person will you be? What kind of faith in God will you have?

Potentially Destructive Core Beliefs

About the World

Life is bad (hard or unfair)
The world is destined to destruct
The world is an unsafe place
People are basically bad
People are out to get me
Life is hard, then you die
Life is unfair
People lie to you
Politicians are all liars
Authorities take advantage
The world owes me a living
It's every person for himself or herself
You simply can't trust people
All stress is bad
To grow old is bad
Things are getting progressively worse
No pain, no gain
The good die young
The world is doomed

About Yourself

I don't fit in
I'm not worthwhile
I'm a loser
I never do things right
I'm not accepted for who I am
I hate my body
I don't deserve love
Things will never work right for me
I'm not supposed to have fun
It's not OK to feel good
I should hide my feelings

I'm such a klutz
I'm not respected
I'm clumsy (ugly, stupid)
Murphy's Law was written about me
I don't do it
To be approved of is everything
I must agree to be accepted
I'm not creative (I can't sing, draw, or do math)
I'll never be happy
I'm not loving (or lovable)
I fail no matter how hard I try
If I suffer, it means I'm no good
I can never live up to my expectations
I ruin everything I touch

About Relationships

People don't understand me
Relationships are tough
Relationships don't last
Friends ultimately fail you
I'm poor at communication
I have lousy luck at love
Men/Women only use you
Good relationships are all luck
If I love I'll be hurt
I'll never find the right person
People take all of your energy
It's my job to improve others
If you depend on people, they'll let you down
People are weak and must be defended
Sex is a weapon (bribe, joke, necessity)
Divorce is a failure (sin, sign I'm a bad person, serves me right)
If you really knew me, you'd hate me
People are basically bad
Take all you can get
What have you done for me lately?
People can't be trusted
My spouse can't get by without me
I can't get by without my spouse
Family comes before me
If I'm not beautiful (thin, rich, smart), then I'm nothing
I can't attract attractive people
Don't get over it, get even

My parents must approve my friends (spouse, career, choices)

Love things, use people

Romance and fun are for the young

About Work

Everyone is out to get you

Do your best, but it won't be good enough

Everything (everyone) has its price

Do unto others, first

People are after my money

Employees are bloodsuckers

Employers are slave drivers

I don't deserve success

Get by as easily as you can

Work harder than everyone else

No one's good work is ever appreciated

Work is never done

Always do better

You are only as good as the work you do

Potentially Useful Phrases

I love myself

I can forgive myself

I am lovable because I am here

God loves me

I deserve to feel good

The love I give to others I can also give to myself

I am a worthy person

My love comes from me

I have the right to live

I have the right to be happy

I can be fair to myself

I am my own best friend

I'm not perfect and that's OK

I generally do my best

The world is safe and friendly

I have choices

I can be gentle with myself

I am one of a kind

There is nothing I must do to be loved

I can accept responsibility for myself

I have internal resources
I can be patient with myself
I can ask for what I need for myself
I choose to love, understand, and heal
I choose love instead of fear
Where I am now is perfect for growth
I enjoy the present moment
What (where, who) I am is OK
Problems can be solved
I am beautiful
I create the experience of love in my life
I can let others love me the way I am
I feel good doing the things I do best
I choose a life of purpose, meaning, and fulfillment
I enjoy but do not need others' approval
I can accept the past
I can welcome the future
I can see beauty in all life
I deserve joy
I bring out the best in others
Love is more important than work
My life is unfolding
I appreciate myself
I deserve to be healthy
I don't need to be sick to be nurtured
My continued guilt doesn't help anyone
I am not a victim
I deserve a loving relationship
I can accept praise
What other people think is their problem
I can learn to feel loved
I do not need my mother's approval
I can live a nurturing, creative life
I can forgive ______________
I am open to new forms of being acknowledged
I no longer have to be angry (hostile, hurt, sad)
I can accept imperfection in others
I can accept my feelings
I can separate people's positive intentions from their negative actions
I am forgiven for my past
I love others unconditionally
I can accept my father's positive intentions
I am the source of my security

I'm into feedback, not failure
I can support myself with my own love
I am in touch with my feelings
I appreciate myself more every day
I enjoy learning and growing
I care for my body lovingly
I watch out for my interests
I can mentally (spiritually, socially) grow indefinitely
I handle my fears capably
I give love and support with no strings attached

Every person you witness to has a combination of beliefs represented by the lists above. The highly skilled witness works with the current belief system that is presented to him or her. Be sensitive to the language and the responses you get so that you may be helpful as a result of how the other is responding. It is also very important for you to become aware of your own beliefs and why you have them.

The spiritually intelligent person builds strong, healthy beliefs. This process occurs throughout the person's lifetime. The person uses excellent self-talk and does her or his best to instill positive beliefs about herself or himself, God and others.

After reading this chapter you might want to take a serious look at your own belief system and how it affects your own witness or even the ability to witness to others at all.

Just a warning: life commandments can have unintended consequences. For example, one of the life commandments that is currently taught to our children is "Don't trust a stranger" or "Beware of strangers." We teach this because we want our children to be able to protect themselves. It is appropriate when they are children. However, if that belief resides into adulthood we will get massive resistance from church members when we say that they should share their faith with someone they do not know. How does this affect you?

The ability to be a witness is so crucial to the church that if we stop doing it the church will lose its focus on bringing people to the love of God. Share your story. Share it in little bits or share it with all the gusto you can. Let people know that God loves them.

STEP II

Pray Deeply: Dialogue with God

One of the most important things I discovered from spiritually intelligent persons that I interviewed was the skills, experiences, and practices of their prayer life. Without exception, prayer was one of the most consistent expressions of their spirituality. It was not just that they prayed but that their prayer experiences were expressed in the form of a dialogue with God. That is, they not only talked with God, but God talked back. They, in fact, had an ongoing relationship.

This is not new for any person who has read the Scriptures. Just read any of the prophets and you will hear the conversations that they had with God. Often there are phrases that occur over and over. For example, in Jeremiah the most repeated phrase is "This is what the Lord Almighty, the God of Israel, says" (for example, in Jeremiah 35:18b), and then Jeremiah states what he has heard. There are many such cases in Jeremiah. In other words, it is not just that Jeremiah talked to God, but God talked back. It is true in the New Testament as well. In Acts 18:9-10 we have an example of God speaking to Paul in a vision. "One night the Lord spoke to Paul in a vision: 'Do not be afraid; keep on speaking, do not be silent. For I am with you, and no one is going to attack and harm you, because I have many people in this city'" (NIV).

If you study the Scriptures closely you will find that there are at least four ways that God directly communicates to us humans. There are many indirect ways as well. The very thought that the God who created the universe with all of its diversity can and will talk—that is, communicate with you and me as individuals—still pushes my faith to its limit. Just think, there are about six and a half billion persons on the Earth. We speak in some six thousand different languages, yet God can speak to each individual in his or her own language and cultural context.

What Is Prayer?

My training in prayer skills has come from two persons who have highly influenced me on my prayer journey. The Right Reverend Michael Pennington, from the Anglican Church in Perth, Australia, has been a great influence for much of my prayer life. Michael has invited me many times to come to his diocese to train his people and others from the western area of Australia. His approach was life changing for me. He introduced me to ways of prayer and meditation that I never knew possible.

The second is the Reverend Kerry Reed, senior pastor of Gender Road Christian Church in Canal Winchester, Ohio. Kerry has taught me the prayers of the ancients, the great prayers of the saints, since they present not only great models for how deeply spiritual persons found their way to God but also how the saints opened their lives to God's love and lived out that love in their everyday lives. I am grateful to both of these deeply spiritual men.

So What Is Prayer?

Let us start with two words: *surdus* and *audire*. *Surdus* is the Latin root "to be deaf," and *audire* is the Latin root "to hear," so prayer is the act of moving from being deaf to the ability to hear. How better could I say it? It is equivalent to "I was blind but now I see." In Mark 4:9 Jesus says, "Let anyone with ears to hear listen!" Prayer is not just our communication with God but God's response back to us. It is from the absurd to the obedient, from not believing to believing with all your heart, mind, and soul. Prayer, in fact, is a movement, a process. It is not just content (words) but a way of living. Thus Paul can say, "Pray without ceasing."

Prayer takes a person from immaturity to maturity—from putting away childish things and becoming the adult. As Paul says in 1 Corinthians 13:11-13:

> When I was a child, I spoke like a child, I thought like a child, I reasoned like a child; when I became an adult, I put an end to childish ways. For now we see in a mirror, dimly, but then we will see face to face. Now I know only in part; then I will know fully, even as I have been fully known. And now faith, hope, and love abide, these three; and the greatest of these is love.

Please note the movements within these verses:

1. from child to adult
2. see in a mirror indirectly, then face to face
3. know in part, then be fully known

Let us at least consider prayer as a movement that brings us closer to God, helps us become mature, responsible Christians, and brings us fully into the world as members of heaven brought down to earth.

Remember Matthew 6:10: "Your will be done, /on earth as it is in heaven." So often we think that prayer is a set of requests that we make of God. Yes, we do make requests, we do have petitions that we make, but it is so much more than this. I hope that the strategies that follow will help you in your spiritual movement.

Poetry often expresses an idea better than logical thought. Here is an inscription found in the ruins of a medieval English convent:

Be silent, still aware,
For there in your heart
The Spirit of prayer
Listen and learn,
Seek and find
Heart, wisdom, Christ

Indirect Ways in Which God Communicates with Us

Nature

Almost any person who has even the most elementary relationship with God will acknowledge that she is often inspired by the beauty and awesomeness of nature. Everything from the pillar of fire in the story of the promised land–seeking Israelites to the teachings of Jesus about the sparrow and the lilies of the field represents such settings. Seeing the beauty of a sunset or sunrise, the power of a waterfall, the rustling of leaves in a warm breeze, or the majesty of an eagle soaring overhead—in all these things God speaks to us.

Several years ago, while doing a training event on Mercer Island outside of Seattle, a member of my group asked if I would like to take some time (I had a day off while being with them) to go look for eagles. I had never seen an eagle in the wild and agreed to journey with him in a boat down one of the nearby rivers.

We set out on a cold, cloudy day, maneuvering the boat to the center of the river. My friend turned off the motor and left us to silently float with the current. We spoke quietly with each other during the first few minutes and then we both became silent and focused our attention on the open sky between the riverbanks and the barren, leafless trees. After some twenty minutes of seeing no eagles, he pointed to a spot high in one of the trees. There was my first glimpse of an eagle. Then my friend quickly pointed to the riverbank where another eagle was pulling away the flesh of a salmon. As we floated, silently, during the next hour and thirty minutes, I enjoyed the cool breeze on my cheeks, and counted forty-two such eagle sightings. It was an experience of being invited into the Holy of Holies in God's creation. You know those events, the standing on the edge of the Grand Canyon or Niagara Falls, the walking in the seven-foot-high cornstalks in a field that seems to have no end, or the rainbow after a warm summer rain. Or maybe you've experienced this walking alone during a cold, still evening when the snow comes gently down, and you stick your tongue out and catch a flake and taste the purity of God's creation. These moments seem special to us. God seems to be close because God is represented in creation.

Please be aware that God is represented. Creation reflects the Creator, but God is not the creation. To believe that God is nature is called animism, that is, worshiping nature rather than the God who created it.

Scriptures

Another form of indirect communication is the Scriptures. You may want to fight with me about that, so let me explain what I mean. God *is* revealed in the Scriptures, but it is indirect.

Let us imagine for a moment that you get a letter from a loved one about how much he loves you. He expresses his affection with genuinely beautiful language. He talks about how important you are to him and the impact you have had on his life. Actually, if you got a letter like that you would most likely cherish it and save it. Assume that you get several letters expressing great fondness and compassion. You are thrilled with the information. But one day you meet the letter writer in person, but he never says those things in that language directly to you. He does not hold your face in his hands and say, "I love you." He only puts this sentiment in some form of writing. Isn't there a difference between the letters and the direct communication?

The same is true with reading Scripture. God can speak to us through Scripture, but it is indirect communication. This does not diminish in any way the power of the Scriptures for us; it is just a way that God communicates with us. The Bible is not God any more than nature is God. The direct way would be to hear the voice of God say, "John, I love you." We will explore more of this later in this chapter.

God and Music

This past Christmas, my wife and I joined other friends to go to a concert at Capital University in Columbus, Ohio. This was about the tenth concert we'd attended with these same friends. The music presented by the choral groups and orchestra was beyond excellent. I sat, after the first several numbers, with every cell of my body responding to the words and marvelous sounds made by these extraordinary voices. I turned to my wife between songs and said that this is what it must be like to be in the heavenly choir. I cried tears prompted by the music's inspiration. Emotions washed over me like a blanket of God's grace and love. Yes, the music was an instrument for my awareness of God. The music was not God any more than nature was God, but it awakened me to God's presence.

Art

Art, even the movies, can bring God's presence close. Several years ago when the movie *The Matrix* came to the theaters, my son Steve called and said, "Hey, Dad, have you seen *The Matrix*? If not, you should. It is filled with lots of scenes that suggest resurrection themes." And sure enough, when Neo is shot to death in the virtual-reality hallway inside the Matrix, his beloved girlfriend kisses the real Neo in the Matrix booth and virtual-reality Neo in the hallway returns to life. So once again in film or theater, the love of God can come through to give us in many forms and events of our live. They wake us up to God's presence if you will pay attention to them.

My wife will sometimes say that she is reluctant to go to the movies with me because I am forever finding God in the film. Again you have to realize that religious and spiritual themes run though much of our literature, plays, dances, and many other artistic forms of our culture. It has been so for a very long time. In some ways it is the process that God uses to communicate with us without naming who God is. Art can serve as an indirect form of revelation.

Direct Ways in Which God Communicates with Us

God Can Talk with Us

"Speak, LORD, for your servant is listening." Earlier in this chapter I mentioned that one of the most direct ways that God communicates with us is by talking with us. That is, God uses language, tone, and syntax to communicate messages to us as if a human friend were standing next to us. Almost all of the people whom I interviewed had this experience many times. Some were profoundly gifted with the sense of God's voice; others, only on occasion.

It is important to note that this gift, skill, or whatever you wish to call it, is not always present in persons who are pursuing spirituality. My wife is a very spiritual person, but she has only heard God's voice indirectly.

Several years ago my wife was asked to be the president of the congregation. She asked what I thought about it, and I suggested that she pray and listen to what God might say about it to her. The next morning when she awoke, she lay still and began to think of some of the things that she might do as president. I asked her what they might be and she shared some of them with me. She said she had never had those thoughts before. I said, "No kidding, I wonder where they came from?" She got the message. She had heard from God. I have found that the communication from God may not be in an audible voice but a unique thought might come to mind unexpectantly—a thought that you never had before. Nurture that by listening for God and the thought can become a voice.

God-given Vision

The Scriptures are loaded with examples of people having visions either in their dreams at night or in a form of trance.

Probably one of the most well-known is that of Peter. In Peter's vision a sheet is lowered down with all kinds of animals in it. And God tells him to eat. This is a great story because had it not taken place I, as a Gentile, might never become a Christian at all. The message of the story is that all are welcome in the kingdom of God. This communication from God allowed Peter to go to the home of Cornelius (a Gentile) and baptize the household into the faith. As a result of Peter's dream (vision) the gospel spread to other people outside the Jewish community.

Here is the actual text:

> In Caesarea there was a man named Cornelius, a centurion of the Italian Cohort, as it was called. He was a devout man who feared God with all his household; he gave alms generously to the people and prayed constantly to God. One afternoon at about three o'clock he had a vision in which he clearly saw an angel of God coming in and saying to him, "Cornelius." He stared at him in terror and said, "What is it, Lord?" He answered, "Your prayers and your alms have ascended as a memorial before God. Now send men to Joppa for a certain Simon who is called Peter; he is lodging with Simon, a tanner, whose house is by the seaside." When the angel who spoke to him had left, he called two of his slaves and a devout soldier from the ranks of those who served him, and after telling them everything, he sent them to Joppa.
>
> About noon the next day, as they were on their journey and approaching the city, Peter went up on the roof to pray. He became hungry and wanted something to eat; and while it was being prepared, he fell into a trance. He saw the heaven opened and something like a large sheet coming down, being lowered to the ground by its four corners. In it were all kinds of four-footed creatures and reptiles and birds of the air. Then he heard a voice saying, "Get up, Peter; kill and eat." But Peter said, "By no means, Lord; for I have never eaten anything that is profane or unclean." The voice said to him again, a second time, "What God has made clean, you must not call profane." This happened three times, and the thing was suddenly taken up to heaven.

> Now while Peter was greatly puzzled about what to make of the vision that he had seen, suddenly the men sent by Cornelius appeared. They were asking for Simon's house and were standing by the gate. They called out to ask whether Simon, who was called Peter, was staying there. While Peter was still thinking about the vision, the Spirit said to him, "Look, three men are searching for you. Now get up, go down, and go with them without hesitation; for I have sent them." So Peter went down to the men and said, "I am the one you are looking for; what is the reason for your coming?" They answered, "Cornelius, a centurion, an upright and God-fearing man, who is well spoken of by the whole Jewish nation, was directed by a holy angel to send for you to come to his house and to hear what you have to say." So Peter invited them in and gave them lodging.
>
> The next day he got up and went with them, and some of the believers from Joppa accompanied him. (Acts 10:1-23)

There are a number of important factors in this story. First, there are several ways that God communicated to different people. "One afternoon at about three o'clock he had a vision in which he clearly saw an angel of God coming in and saying to him. . . ." Peter then had his experience:

> He fell into a trance. He saw the heaven opened and something like a large sheet coming down, being lowered to the ground by its four corners. In it were all kinds of four-footed creatures and reptiles and birds of the air. Then he heard a voice saying, "Get up, Peter; kill and eat." But Peter said, "By no means, Lord; for I have never eaten anything that is profane or unclean." The voice said to him again, a second time, "What God has made clean, you must not call profane." This happened three times, and the thing was suddenly taken up to heaven. (Acts 10:9-16)

Please note that these events happened in broad daylight; this is not a night dream. Peter does not mutely respond to God's command, but he argues with God, insisting on his own way, that he should not do it. And then something wonderful happened. A new thought, a new understanding, a new revelation, a new command, with a visual image attached, occurred to Peter that had never occurred before. For now all the rules that Peter had followed in the past were about to be abandoned. This is the stuff of revolutionary change. This story has all the components of the communicating God. It is auditory, visual, and experiential. It breaks old patterns and creates a new way of being. The consequence was that the faith in Christ brought new hope to all the people, even Gentiles.

God also spoke to Samuel:

> Samuel was lying down in the temple of the LORD, where the ark of God was. Then the LORD called, "Samuel! Samuel!" and he said, "Here I am!" and ran to Eli, and said, "Here I am, for you called me." But he said, "I did not call; lie down again." So he went and lay down. The LORD called again, "Samuel!" Samuel got up and went to Eli, and said, "Here I am, for you called me." But he said, "I did not call, my son; lie down again." Now Samuel did not yet know the LORD, and the word of the LORD had not yet been revealed to him. The LORD called Samuel again, a third time. And he got up and went to Eli, and said, "Here I am, for you called me." Then Eli perceived that the LORD was calling the boy. Therefore Eli said to Samuel, "Go, lie down; and if he calls you, you shall say, 'Speak, LORD, for your servant is listening.'" So Samuel went and lay down in his place.
>
> Now the LORD came and stood there, calling as before, "Samuel! Samuel!" And Samuel said, "Speak, for your servant is listening." Then the LORD said to Samuel, "See, I am about to do something in Israel that will make both ears of anyone who hears of it tingle." (1 Samuel 3:3-11)

Such a wonderful story. Note the phrase "Now Samuel did not yet know the LORD, and the word of the LORD had not yet been revealed to him." So God can call us even if we don't understand what the voice is all about. Then someone like Eli has to make us aware and tell us to listen and respond. That's how it is, folks, listen and respond.

The spiritually attentive person has developed the sensitivity to hear and pay attention to the inner voice. These persons trust themselves and God enough to respond.

Several years ago I had the honor of being the spiritual leader for a retreat with 140 Anglican priests in New Zealand. We started the retreat with twelve hours of silence. Even at meals there was no talking. In the afternoon I took a walk to meditate and pray. Behind the chapel, where we worshiped together, there was a pasture with sheep silently grazing. There was a path that led to the wire fence and a set of steps had been built over the fence so you could walk through the pasture. (Sheep cannot climb steps so no worry about them getting out.) I climbed the steps and entered the path that guided me to the other side of the field where another set of steps allowed me to leave the pasture. As I continued on the path I entered the "bush," a grouping of very high bushes on both sides of the path. It was a clear, beautiful day, with a cool breeze. The only sound was the movement of the leaves in the bushes and the sounds of singing birds, when in a startling moment I heard a voice say, "Hi John, want to talk?" I knew immediately who it was and replied, "Hi, God. Sure, let's talk." "What do you want to talk about today?" asked the voice. And off goes the conversation. I share the opening part of that conversation with you because I will remember what happened for the rest of my life.

John: God, I want to ask you a question that I have never asked you before.

God: Sure. You know you can ask me any question. What's on your mind?

John: How are you, God? What's it like to be God?

God: I am love. John, that's what I am. That's how I am. I love you, John, and I love everyone who I have created with the same love; no more, no less. I love my creation; I love those I have created. Now I have a question for you, John.

John: *"Uh-oh," I said to myself as if I could hide it from God. Here it comes, a question back from God.* What's the question?

God: Do you love me as much as I love you?

John: You should know the answer to that, since you know my heart.

God: Yes, I do, but do you?

John: I do love you, Lord, but not as much as you love me.

God: Why not? Don't you love me with all your heart, mind, and soul?

John: With my heart, yes, with my soul, yes, with my mind—there is where I have a problem. I do not hold you in my mind all the time; I do not pray without ceasing as Paul did. I am better at it, but I struggle with my mind.

God: And John, do you love others as I love them?

John: I am not sure I know how to do that. How do you love over 6 billion people at the same time?

And so the dialogue went on for over thirty minutes.

The developing of this dialogical skill set takes patience, and a process of being alert to not only what is going on in your head and body but also that which is surrounding you. But any communication is always God's gracious gift. No matter how much practicing you do, there is no guarantee that God will talk to you in this way. I'm still not sure why God picked me in this way. But remember that God is communicating with you in some way all the time, it's just that you are not always aware of it. So practice daily being attentive. Listen for the voice that brings healing and wholeness. You will be surprised how God shows up in your life.

Angels

There are other visual representations of God, some of which are God's angels who communicate God's message in a variety of ways, both day and night. Sometimes the Bible is unclear if it is God or an angel who speaks.

Joseph had such an experience after the birth of Jesus. While the Bible indicates that the text spoken is that of an angel, the text actually says that the Lord warned Joseph in a dream. As a result of that communication, Joseph took his wife, Mary, and child, Jesus, to Egypt to escape Herod's order to kill all infants under two years of age near and around Bethlehem: "After they had gone, an angel of the Lord appeared to Joseph in a dream, and said, 'Get up, take the child and his mother and escape with them to Egypt, and stay there until I tell you; for Herod is going to search for the child to kill him.' So Joseph got up, took mother and child by night, and sought refuge with them in Egypt" (Matthew 2:13-14 REB).

God Can Give You a Passion

Without exception the persons I interviewed exuded energy and passion for the ministries that they were doing. Their spirituality was not limited to some pious form of behavior but showed itself in great activity in the communities and congregations in which they were engaged. This does not mean that they were without conflict or anxiety about what they were doing. In fact, the very passion often got them into issues with their religious groups. One pastor got into trouble because he wanted his church to be open to all, including homosexuals. He took the story of Peter's dream quite literally "All are clean." Others did not agree. A nun wanted to help in the merger of different orders of nuns, and after much struggle she was part of a group that achieved the combining of different orders into one group. There is a price that is paid for such commitment and assertiveness.

During interaction with these people, I found myself energized just by being with them. Not only were they able to talk about their relationship with God but how that relationship expressed itself as a witness to the world. Later in this book I will explore the process of translating the faith into action.

We understand today that passion is the energy we have for a given mission or task. It is the excitement and enthusiasm for life. It may be surprising to you, but one of the most frequent ways that God communicates with us is in the experience of that passion. Since we are experiencing many things in a given day, our awareness that God is in the experience allows us to pay attention to each event as a place where God can be known to us.

There are dramatic shifts of passion that can take place where God is in the shift. This very day as I write this page, I have been in conversation with a wonderful pastor who has experienced such a shift and knows that God was in the process. She had earned her PhD in English and taught English at a university for twenty-five years. Then her passions began to shift. That which had made her so successful was now moving into discomfort and boredom. It was in that shift that she recognized that God was moving her to a new relationship and with a new purpose. She is now pastor of a small urban church. Such shifts of passion are not unusual. I have experienced those shifts myself. I was a pastor for twenty-six years. I loved it and then the shift began to take place. What used to drive me when I got up in the morning began to wane. I shall never forget it, though it is many years behind me. I began to think more and more about doing consulting and training for my own denomination. I was pulled apart inside because I did not want to leave the passion I had for the congregation. Yet I was giving more thought to the trainer part of me.

I remember one summer evening I walked out on a grassy lawn outside the camp at which I was doing training in listening skills. I was still pastor of my church, but I had also started to do some training with groups both in and out of my own denomination. I prayed to God/Christ to give me some direction. What should I do? Stay in the ministry of the congregation or expand my training to the larger world? In my agony—experience—I cried to God: "Tell me what to do." Then the voice came back, clear as a bell: "John, I am not going to tell you what to do anymore. You decide what you want to do for me for the rest of your life; whatever you decide will be OK. But you decide." I said, "God, that isn't fair. You are to tell me what to do so I can do your will." I will never forget the answer I got back: "John, grow up, make your own decisions. I will be in that decision with you." It has been that way ever since.

My experience will not be your experience. Yours may be quite different. I am just saying to trust your own experience.

Experience Your Experiences

I have discovered a profound process in all of this: most people do not experience their experiences; they either ignore them, refuse to feel them, or reject them. Because God communicates with you in your experiences, you then shut out a lot of what God may want to communicate to you. Instead, allow yourself to feel the feelings of the experience.

In a wonderful book titled *The Practice of the Presence of God*, Brother Lawrence shares a marvelous insight:

> When he began his work, he said to God, with a filial trust in Him:
>
> "O my God, since Thou art with me, and I must now, in obedience to They commands, apply my mind to these outward things. I beseech Thee to grant me the grace to continue in Thy presence; and to this end do Thou prosper me with Thy assistance, receive all my works, and possess all my affections."
>
> As he proceeded in his work, he continued his familiar conversation with his Maker, imploring His grace, and offering to Him all his action.
>
> When he had finished, he examined himself how he had discharged his duty.
>
> If he found (he had done it) well. He returned thanks to God.
>
> If otherwise, he asked pardon and, without being discouraged, he set his mind right again, and continued his exercise of the presence of God as if he had never deviated from it.[1]

I love this sentence: "I beseech Thee to grant me the grace to continue in Thy presence; and to this end do Thou prosper me with Thy assistance, receive all my works, and possess all my affections."

This is the perfect example of what I mean when I say that God is in all that we do. You just have to wake up to the experience. Or as Brother Lawrence put it: "My time of business does not with me differ from the time of prayer. In the noise and clatter of my kitchen, while several persons are at the same time called for different things, I possess God in as great tranquility as if I were on my knees at the Blessed Sacrament."[2]

What Brother Lawrence is trying to teach all of us, Protestant, Catholic, Jew, or Muslim, is that there should be no difference in your relationship with God when you are in worship than when you are at work. God is present in it all. If we had a deep understanding of this we would not be fighting and killing people in the name of God.

Brother Lawrence had an unusual ability to be in the presence of God and to communicate with God at a deep personal level. I call that process the ability to dialogue with God.

A Skill Needed to Develop the Ability to Dialogue with God

Dialoguing is a deceptively simple set of two behaviors: listening and sharing. The following is an example of an interpersonal dialogue.

I was on my way to do a training event in Mobile, Alabama. I got on the plane in Columbus, Ohio, and was seated in first class a couple of rows back on the aisle. Seated next to me at the window was a woman dressed in a business suit and scarf, with a small briefcase at her feet. As I put on my seat belt, she said, "Hi"; I said "Hi" back, and off went the dialogical process.

Woman: Where you headed?

John: Atlanta, I hope. (That was where the plane was scheduled to go; I was going to change planes in Atlanta.) How about you?

Woman: Yeah, Atlanta too, my final stop. Is Atlanta your final stop?

John: No, I'm on my way to Mobile, Alabama.

Woman: On a business trip or something else?

John: No, business. I'm teaching a group in listening skills. What takes you to Atlanta?

Woman: It's where I live and work. I'm an executive at one of the TV stations. Tell me about the listening skills workshop that you're doing.

John: I'm working with a congregation there teaching them how to listen to one another. It helps reduce the conflict in the church. It is one of the things that I do most often. Tell me what it's like to be an executive at a TV station.

Woman: I'm in charge of sales, getting clients to pay for TV time. I travel a great deal of the time. You travel a lot too?

John: Yeah, I'm on the road about two hundred days a year. How about you?

Woman: That beats me. I'm away maybe a hundred days.

And so went the conversation, which lasted the hour and twenty minutes that it took to fly to Atlanta.

If you look at this conversation, you will note two important things. The question that is asked is answered and then asked back to the person who asked it. It gives the person an opportunity to answer your question and then have the opportunity to ask. In this way two people can find parallel experiences otherwise known as common ground. It is one of the most thoughtful and affirming behaviors I have observed from those who know how to listen and share. It is in fact so simple, yet one of the most difficult things to do. If you know how to dialogue but the other person does not, then the dialogue stops.

It is difficult because most of the time while someone is talking with a person, that person is not thinking of a question (or even actually listening), but is thinking of what to say when the other person stops talking. And most of the time it is not even on the same subject. Dialogical prayer is made up of the same process; it is not just you talking, or requesting what you want from God, but is the act of making your statement and then listening for a response. In the next chapter, on meditation and reflection, I will explore the many ways that dialogical prayer can be developed and maintained.

A Time to Practice

Take time to be still and listen to your own thoughts and the dialogue that you have with yourself. One of those voices in you may be God's. Sorting that out is not always easy, but there is a criterion that I use to know if it is God's voice and not one of the many that are in my head. Let me clarify what I mean by voices in your head. First, I am not talking about schizophrenia, which is a mental disorder "where hallucinations consist of a voice keeping up a running commentary on the person's behavior or thoughts, or two or more voices conversing with each other."[3] The average healthy person talks to him or herself hundreds of time a day. It is simply called thinking, meditating, musing. If we say what we are thinking then we share our insights, concerns, feelings and thoughts. When God communicated to those I interviewed, it was as both a thought and sometimes an audible voice that came to the person's awareness. Now, how do you know it is God's voice and not some other voice of your thinking. This is my criteria. God's voice is life giving and enhancing. It is uplifting and brings you the fullness of life. It is full of grace, love, and acceptance. God's voice is not hostile or violent. Remember: God loves you, and there is nothing you can do to stop it. I frequently go by a United Church of Christ building and a sign says "God is still talking. Are you listening?" This happens to be the current theme of the UCC.

Learning to trust that thought/voice takes practice. Respond to it the best you can and then be aware of what happens. Do not be afraid to talk back to it, or converse with it. You may be as surprised at what you get as Peter or the Prophets were.

Exercise I: Centering Prayer

Here is an exercise to help you begin to listen. This form of prayer requires from ten to twenty minutes of silent time, although you can start with less time. There are a number of steps to this prayer form. You do not have to be perfect with them, but as you practice you will find them to become more natural and available to you. (I am following the form of Fr. Thomas Keating, who has perfected this strategy.)

First: Sit down in a comfortable chair and take several deep breaths to relax your body and mind.

Second: Choose a sacred word as the symbol of your intention to consent to God's presence and action. The sacred word can be words like *love*, *forgiveness*, *peace*, *patience*, *hope*, and so forth. It is a word of your choice. It represents your intention to be in God's presence, and that is what is important in the choice you make. Please note that it is not just the word but the action that may come from it after focusing (centering) on that word.

Third: As you sit comfortably, settle on the sacred word and silently introduce the sacred word that symbolizes the *consent* of your will to be in God's presence and action within.

Finally: During this time of centering on your sacred word, extraneous thoughts may enter into your thinking—sort of like background music in a grocery store. Pay little attention to them and engage in your thoughts and ever so gently return to the sacred word.

In some forms of prayer the additional thoughts are to be

rejected. In centering prayer, they are a part of the milieus (context) in which the sacred word shows up. The intention of the word is to bring you into the awareness of God's presence, to expand your fellowship with God and then help you initiate some kind of action you think is required as a result of such a relationship. The power of centering prayer is not just the experience you may have, but the outcome of such an experience.

Centering prayer can be used in many settings, either by yourself or with a group. In my experience of meeting with a group of spiritual directors and spiritual supervisors, we almost always start our time together with centering prayer as a way of preparing our relationship with God and with the work we must do with one another. There are more prayer and meditation exercises in the next chapter.

STEP III

Simplify Your Desires: Learn to Meditate, Reflect, and Contemplate

Here, again, are the spiritual intelligences that I found in my research. I believe that naming them again in a slightly different way will help you see the logical flow and progression of steps to spiritual maturity. It will help you see how the steps work together. You may want to underline key words so that you can better remember them.

Step I: The skill and ability to state what you believe about God, others, and yourself. This entails sharing with another your own story, what has happened to you in your personal journey—the ability to be a witness.

Step II: The ability to dialogue with God in prayer. This includes skills associated with listening.

Step III: The disciplines of meditation, reflection, and contemplation. These disciplines will help you simplify your life.

Step IV: The willingness to face your challenges, to be stripped down inside so that internal struggles can be used to build character and understanding. This is the creative use of spiritual desert time.

Step V: The passion to be in mission for others and to share oneself with the world. The continual studying of the Scriptures and the ability to find meaning in all things and events of your life will expand your understanding.

Said another way, spiritually intelligent Christians are those who share their faith with other persons. They are persons who have an intimate relationship (prayer life) with God; they have disciplines of reflection and spend time in meditation; they can enter their deepest struggles and pain and emerge the stronger for it. They are in mission for others and commit themselves to be a lifelong learner of the spiritual disciplines, including the study of Scripture. And they have the ability to search diligently for meaning and purpose in all of life's experiences.

Learn to Meditate, Reflect, and Contemplate

Step III in the process of spiritual development is the ability to learn how to meditate—to stay focused on God's presence; reflect—to find your purpose through everyday events; and contemplate—to find meaning in all of life's experiences. In this part of the book I will address how to deepen your relationship with God through these methods. For some this may be very familiar; for others it may be the first time you have ever encountered these ideas. Because I have worked with much of the Christian-faith spectrum, I am aware how different denominations and faith orientations respond to the ideas of meditation and reflection. The liturgical churches tend to be more familiar with these concepts; yet I have interviewed many persons in the free traditions and the very conservative faith orientations who know how and why it is important to develop these spiritual skills and behaviors.

The very fact that these skills are known throughout the history of the Christian faith makes them powerful. In their most elementary way, meditation and reflection are simply ways of paying attention to how God shows up around you each day of your life. Or as Elizabeth Barrett Browning wrote:

> Earth's crammed with heaven,
> And every common bush afire with God;
> And only he who sees takes off his shoes.[1]

Meditation is the ability to prepare your heart for prayer. Meditation leads you into the presence of God where you may experience God in a more intimate way. You do not have to meditate to pray, but it is like holding a loved one's hands, looking into that person's eyes before you say, "I love you." Certainly, you can say "I love you" in other ways, but there is something wonderful about being with your loved one. Meditation is preparation to be with God.

Meditation can be done just for its own sake. To meditate on an object, like a flower, or to select a passage of Scripture for which you seek its deeper message may also be enriching in and of itself. So, basically, meditation is the process of paying attention to God and not wandering off with a hundred other thoughts. Simple to say, more difficult to do. To wake up to your thoughts, feelings, hopes, dreams, and sorrows is not always easy. But to find God in those things is enlivening. So to meditate is to come alive.

Georgia Harkness, in her book on prayer, says that

> God does not expect us to approach him with an empty mind. There are extremes to be avoided, for God does not make himself known best either in a vacuum or in a welter of our own or another's thoughts. One discovers God and his will by patient, quiet focusing of attention in this direction. The purpose of meditation is not merely to make one think. Thinking in the speculative or problem-solving sense may well recede at this point. To meditate upon God is to think about God and his great goodness, his never failing care, our place in his Kingdom, what he requires of us. Without such meditation prayer is apt to degenerate either into self-centered clamorous petition or into a vague form of aimless, comfortable musing.[2]

Meditation can be and often is the bridge to prayer, but it can also be used to explore the deeper meaning of many things. Here are some ways to do this. Even though I have talked about prayer in the previous chapter, I would like to extend that discussion.

A Setting for Meditation and Reflection

When you are beginning your journey with meditation, there are settings that help you get started. They are not mandatory but are often helpful.

- A quiet environment: As difficult as this may be for you, try to find a quiet place and time. After the kids have gone to bed, and the TV is off, snuggle into your favorite chair and relax. Just be still for a moment—it does not have to be a long time, particularly when you are just getting started.
- An object to dwell on, whether a word or a symbol: This may be a word from the Scriptures, a favorite picture of your children, a picture of Jesus, or a photo from your last vacation. This will get you to focus and help you resist distractions.

- A comfortable position: Let the chair, or whatever you are sitting on, be the place for your entire weight. It should make you aware that you are being held by something, like a swing or the back of a chair.
- A passive attitude: Relax, let the muscles go loose, take a deep breath, and you have created the setting for our first exercise.

The following are several meditation exercises. Meditation is often used with free association. Open yourself to new possibilities.

Exercise I: A New Life-Giving Belief System

This exercise is a combination of meditation and contemplation (contemplation is finding meaning in an event or idea). It uses two brief biblical parables of Jesus. They are likely to be familiar. You can use any story of Jesus or his parables upon which to meditate. Remember all prayer, meditation, and so on has one basic function: to bring you closer to God or, more accurately, to wake up to God's presence in your life.

Matthew 13:44: "The kingdom of heaven is like treasure hidden in a field, which someone found and hid; then in his joy he goes and sells all that he has and buys that field." And Matthew 13:45: "Again, the kingdom of heaven is like a merchant in search of fine pearls; on finding one pearl of great value, he went and sold all that he had and bought it."

Seeking God on the Christian journey is often misunderstood. It is as if we have to find God. The spiritually intelligent persons with whom I talked turned that around for me. They were not in the process of seeking so much as they were in the process of receiving that which was already there. You just had to become aware of it. The treasure is already there.

Many years ago four adults—including me—took twenty-six teenagers to the Holy Land, as well as to Egypt and part of Europe. During our time in the Holy Land, we visited five major archaeological digs. As we were walking toward one of the digs—I brought up the rear to make sure all the kids were with us—I looked down and saw what I thought was a potsherd (broken piece of pottery) barely visible above the ground. I stopped and took a small potsherd that I had found earlier and started to dig about it and discovered it was not a broken piece but an entire pot. I called to the archaeologist who was our guide and he returned with the youth. Together we dug around the pot. We did not remove it from its resting place but were able to see that it was about four feet high. It was lying on its side. The archaeologist was an expert in dating pottery by its shape and size. He looked at it carefully and said that it was about 2,000 years old. We talked about the pot and speculated about who might have made it and why it was buried where it lay. What was carried or stored in it? We used our imaginations and thought about what it could teach us, and the times of its use. We then neatly returned all of the soil back around the pot and covered it. I do not know if anyone else ever found it. But it was a treasure waiting to be found.

In the silence of your journey, when you are alone with God, treasures buried deep within you will come to your awareness. Some people can do this with great power, and when this happens, it is often called the "eureka" moment.

I love to push ideas regarding how God works in our lives and how we often miss the deepest structures of that work when we are reading the Scriptures. Just as the story of the good Samaritan can yield much deeper meanings for us, so these two parables of Jesus can do the same. The point of this process is to reveal to us that which seems impossible. It often is a treasure or pearl that is so profound that you will do everything possible to bring it into your life. What is amazing is that these experiences with God are available to all of us if we will "let" them happen. It is quite difficult to "make" them happen. Some are simple moments of awareness. Others are profound, life-changing awakenings—thoughts or feelings you never knew were there, although they were there, buried deep in the field of our mind and soul.

As seen above, in Matthew 13:44, there is the parable of the hidden treasure: "The kingdom of heaven is like treasure hidden in a field, which someone found and hid; then in his joy he goes and sells all that he has and buys that field." You can imagine that if the person did not look (seek) he would not ever have found the treasure. When we find such an insight or gift are we willing to develop it? If not, we let it sit buried and never bring it to light. What are we willing to give (sell all that we have?) in order to develop it?

My daughter Sandy recently has discovered such a gift in herself, and though it took a considerable sacrifice on her part, she spent most of her money, time, and effort to pursue it. She was an excellent horticulturist but was willing to forfeit that business, at least in part, to follow a new unearthing: going back to college to get a nursing degree. Her husband and children are supportive. This leads to an interesting question. If the seeker was willing to sell all that he had to get the treasure, how did his family feel about such an adventure? We will never know.

It is in sitting silently that you can unearth the gifts that God has given you.

Exercise II: The Hands

This meditation provides you with deep insights about yourself and what you offer to God. It is simple to do. Try it.

Place both of your hands in front of you. First look at the back of your hands—the color, the lines, and the texture. Take one hand and pinch the skin on the back of the other hand. You will notice something significant. If the skin resumes its normal shape rapidly, you still have lots of elasticity left in the skin. This happens probably because you are still young—under fifty—but if you notice that the skin slowly goes back to normal or even just stays in the pinched position, you have lost lots of skin flexibility and you are getting older. Now reflect on what getting older means to you.

Turn your hands over and look at the lines that run across the palms of your hands. There will be at least two or more lines crossing or intersecting each other. I am an exception to those two or more lines. I only have one single line. A doctor told me that that single line shows up in hydrocephalic children. I was not hydrocephalic but was born six weeks prematurely and maybe have some genetic flaw. Please note that my reflection, my meditation on such an event, is significant to me. What do your hands say about you—your life story, your faith story?

Now think of all the places your hands have been; the times when they helped others or the times when you injured or abused someone. Think of their gentleness when they caressed a child's hair or held the hand of someone who grieved. Meditate on your hands. Think of the skills your hands have developed: typing on a computer keyboard, making a wood cabinet, fixing a car, putting a new door on your house, planting flowers, or driving a car. You can name hundreds of things. What comes to mind as you reflect on these things? How can you thank God for your hands—what have they done in the name of God?

Exercise III: Words of Affirmation

What do you say to yourself while you are meditating? If you unearth a gem but then say to yourself, "Oh, I could never do that" or "I am not worthy of such a gift," you will bury it again.

Thus one of the greatest things that could ever happen to you will never see the light of day. So what do you need to say to yourself when you discover such a gift or treasure from God? Practice saying words of affirmation to yourself as you meditate.

I offer only three things here, but mind you, they can generate wonder, hope, and faith. This first is one of those things that was unearthed in my own field, my own life through meditation. It just came to me one day and I have said it hundreds of times since: "I am loved by God, and there is nothing I can do to stop it." At other times I may use the following statement: "God, you have made me and you delight in me. With all my heart I thank you." Or "God, you have shown me that I am of infinite worth."

How can you accept an infinitely wonderful gift if you feel that you yourself are not of infinite value?

There are many more such exercises; they come from the history of spirituality and can be found in many books. Works such as *Prayer and the Common Life* by Georgia Harkness, or *Prayer: Finding the Heart's True Home* by Richard J. Foster, or *The Spiritual Exercises of St. Ignatius of Loyola: A Handbook for Directors* by Marian Cowan and John Carroll Futrell represent a wide range of meditation and prayer styles.

The Context for Meditation and Reflection

When should these spiritual disciplines be practiced? At first they are done at specific times when you can be quiet and alone. However, I am aware that many distractions can get in the way. The kids are running around, the TV is on, and there are countless things to do around the house. And when there is quiet time, like at the end of the day, you sit alone for a few minutes, and because you are tired you start into a meditation and fall asleep.

So consider two ways of meditation (I include contemplation and reflection). One is rather formal, the quiet time alone. The other is meditation-on-the-run and in everything you do. They are both productive.

You are waiting for the kids after the ball game; you can meditate on how God was there, in this place at this time. It does not take long, a few moments, but it wakes you up to God's presence in all events. How is God in the winning or the losing of the game? Reflect on the Bible stories you know where failure took place and how God was present; for example, when Jesus told Peter to walk on the water, Peter started and than sank. How is that story like losing a game? Remember that the ultimate end of meditation is to keep you constantly awake to God's presence in all that you think and do. It leads to Paul's statement in 1 Thessalonians 5:16-18: "Rejoice always, pray without ceasing, give thanks in all circumstances; for this is the will of God in Christ Jesus for you."

Meditation during Difficult Times

I have been a spiritual director for about twelve years. The role of the spiritual director is to help a person find and nurture the best relationship with God during her lifetime. About 90 percent or more of the people who call me to be their director are at that time in some serious spiritual situation. It may seem odd to you, but this is one of the most spiritually productive times, or at least it can be.

This difficult time is often referred to as spiritual desert time and it has certain characteristics. I'll say more about this time in the next chapter. It is brought on by a cluster (a series) of events, and persons often feel as if life is falling apart. It is a time of disorientation, a time of not knowing what to do with your life, and is often accompanied with a shift of passions. You used to love to do what you are currently invested in, but now it feels like you are in a rut—the passion is gone. You can do it, but it feels more like work than fun. It feels heavy and you feel burdened.

One of the common feelings is that you feel stuck. You don't like where you are but you don't see any way out. This is particularly true for clergy who have been in ministry for many years. Their church now only feels like a burden with no exit. The spiritually intelligent persons know about this stage. All of those I interviewed (no exceptions) told me stories of this gut-wrenching time when faith seemed like shifting sand and God seemed distant or nonexistent.

I sat with a pastor while doing training in Florida. We came to a break in the training when he asked me if we could speak. We were standing in the corner of the room and he just slid down the wall onto the floor. His behavior told me more than his words ever could. He was cornered and he couldn't get up. He told me that he had been a pastor for over twenty years. He was in a terrible place spiritually because, as he put it, "I preach about God every Sunday but I no longer believe there is one. What do I do?" Surely the man is in desert time, the time when there is dryness of faith. This is the time when the securities of faith and life seem to be sifting away. It feels terrible for most people. It is frightening and disillusioning. Most people want to avoid it like a plague. Yet it can be one of the most powerful, spiritually expanding times of your life. In fact, we now know that, for the growing Christian, this stage of faith occurs approximately every five to seven years. Sometimes the desert time is short and relatively nonstressful, but other times it shakes you to your core, and makes you question everything you have ever believed. You can become cynical about the church, what it has taught you, and what you believe. Here is where meditation and particularly reflection can be helpful even if it is disconcerting.

Meditation and journaling are useful skills, and all you have to do is go to the Bible to find the perfect model for engaging desert times. Turn to the book of Lamentations.

Lamenting is the act of sharing your deepest agony with God even when you are not sure there is one. You can rail against God with all of your anger or despair. This sharing of intense emotion is a way to spend intimate time with God.

The lament has two parts: the anger expressed and the praise given. Below are examples of the language of Lamentations.

> He has walled me about so that I cannot escape;
>   he has put heavy chains on me;
> though I call and cry for help,
>   he shuts out my prayer;
> he has blocked my ways with hewn stones,
>   he has made my paths crooked. (3:7-9)

That is what the stuck state feels like; that is what you might experience when you pray and there is no response.

But the second part of the lament structure is the reaction to this blocking: emptiness time.

> The thought of my affliction and my homelessness
>   is wormwood and gall!
> My soul continually thinks of it
>   and is bowed down within me.
> But this I call to mind,
>   and therefore I have hope:
>
> The steadfast love of the LORD never ceases,
>   his mercies never come to an end;
> they are new every morning;
>   great is your faithfulness.
> "The LORD is my portion," says my soul,
>   "therefore I will hope in him." (3:19-24)

It is the phrase "But this I call to mind" that represents the meditation process. In the desert meditation time there is the opportunity to explore both the doubt (which is the leading edge of new faith) and the affirmations you have made in your life. It is quite all right to sit and ponder the experiences that led you into the desert and those times when life was full of hope. It is an *and* experience—a meditation walk.

Several years ago I was honored to be invited to the ninetieth birthday celebration of Dr. Elton Trueblood (one of the greatest Quaker theologians) at the Yokefellow Training Center in Indiana. A small group of us was sitting in the foyer talking with Dr. Trueblood. I asked him, "If you could say one word that would express your ninety years of life, what would you say?" His response was immediate: "And." Then he added, "Life is an 'and.' It is being healthy and sick, it is faith and doubt and it is joy and sorrow. Life is an 'and' and when you have learned to live in the 'and' of your life you have learned to live." What a wonderful insight from a man with great spiritual intelligence and wisdom. The lament is a powerful "and" statement. It is screaming at God *and* sharing your love for God all at the same time.

In order to meditate in this desert time, it is often helpful to return to the beginnings of your faith. Visualize yourself in some of the beginning development. Return there for a few moments and think of how God was present in the beginning. What of that experience can you use now in guiding you through this unsure time?

What serves as your oasis? Find a place of comfort—to rest for a moment but not stay there. Desert time is a journey; it is not a final place to be. One other thing to do in this time of spiritual growth; go find someone to serve. In that serving you will find yourself moving through difficult times with greater intention and energy.

The comments above came from an individual I interviewed who had been through the desert many times. I hope that you are in a church that will allow you to express your struggle. Often the desert time is not supported with help from your local church. I hope the excerpt from the poem below represents the Christians you have with you on your journey.

If This Is Not a Place

If this is not a place, where tears are understood,
then where shall I go to cry?[3]

Contemplation

Contemplation is a state of mystical awareness of God's being in order to find direction and purpose for your life. It is being in that presence that causes you to change. To contemplate is to enter into the journey with God. It can be taking a Scripture and entering into the story. Find your favorite Scripture. If you don't have one, I suggest the feeding of the four thousand, in Matthew 15:32-39. Be present in the story—feel, smell, hear what is going on. Then become aware of what the story evokes from you. Let the story be your guide and teacher. It will share the genuineness of its truth.

The stories in which Jesus is present are always a fruitful place to begin. What does Jesus have to say to you in the story? What do you say back? Be open to all that is going on—the heat of the sun, the smell of the fields, the noise of the carts on the road. Let the story become a vivid movie in your mind. See Jesus coming to you. Or are you going to him? You are in the presence of Christ—what do you experience? What has been awakened in you? As a result of the experience, what do you want to do?

Contemplation is not a dead end. It is the moving power of being fully alive. As Jesus said, "I came that they may have life, and have it abundantly" (John 10:10).

Desert times are a stage of spirituality that often lies beyond most institutional churches. It is the experience of coming to God through your personal reflection and understanding. This experience and its potential benefits may have never been taught to you by your church. You may have a dream, a vision, a strong feeling; still you question all these experiences and never say anything to anyone for fear that he or she will think you are crazy. So you ignore it and hope it will go away.

It may be that your faith has hit a wall of understanding. You have lost your job, your child has contracted cancer, or your parents have been injured in a car accident. Tragedies may prod you to question many things about your faith. I remember clearly a statement made to us in seminary by our theology professor: "You will have parishioners ask, 'Why did this happen to me?' Your answer is, 'I don't know.' But then you can say, 'Now that it has happened, what are you going to do with the experience?'" You may never find "the why" of an event, but you always have a choice of how you will respond.

Desert experiences are filled with despair *and* hope. So when a person tells me that he is not sure of what he believes about God anymore, I applaud him and say, "Fantastic. Now you are open to other alternatives and understandings of the nature of God." Maybe the old ones do not work anymore. This does not mean that all of your faith is in the process of being altered. On occasion, that might happen. But it is rare. It does mean that a shift is taking place.

Do you remember, earlier in this book, when I shared my experience of making the decision to leave parish ministry and become a consultant and trainer? That was one of my desert times. I struggled for nearly five years and grieved hard when I left my parish. (I loved those people.) Then one day I came out of the desert. I was different and my journey took a turn. I was refreshed and restored.

The desert time I have referred to above ended with a theophanic dream. A theophanic dream is one where God, Christ, or an angel appears to you. In my case, it was Jesus. Please note that the context and experience of this dream are way beyond anything I normally have or even understand. Jesus invited me to say Mass with him. I am not a Roman Catholic; I do not know how to say Mass.

The place where the dream occurred was in a beautiful sanctuary. Jesus was dressed in a monk's robe; I was in street clothes. I agreed to do what he asked and we went through the Mass together—how did I know how to do that? At the end of the Mass, Jesus came to me, fully embraced me, and while holding me whispered in my ear, "John, I love you!" A warmth of love like I had never known before filled me to the brim. It is a feeling of encouragement and hope and being fully forgiven. I awoke and knew that the decisions I had made were the right ones. That event was nearly thirty years ago; yet as I write these lines, my eyes fill with tears and the joy of the memory is still with me.

Desert time is one of struggle that can lead to a new understanding of who you are and what you are to do. It is a time of shifting and reshaping your beliefs for your current life situation. *It is learning to trust God in the not knowing.*

A well-known Bible passage about desert time is found in Genesis 32:22-32. This story talks about Jacob's encounter with an angel, although the language about exactly whom Jacob struggles with is ambiguous. When Jacob awoke he walked away with two things, the two things that desert time produces for the person who engages its power. First, he walked away with a new name: Israel. Desert time helps you find a new identity and a new mission. But, second, he walked away with a limp. There is a cost to desert time. Paradoxically, your wound enables you to heal others. Your wound heals you so that you can better empathize with the hurt and suffering of others. Through contemplation, you can seek to experience God and find marvelous things beyond your current knowing. Sometimes God will provide for you ideas that, at the time, don't make sense. Only when you reflect on what has happened and the decisions you have made will you come to an understanding of how God is at work in your life.

The persons I interviewed all knew about the experience of the "desert." Some knew it by that name; others told of faith struggles and how they moved to a new understanding of God/Christ. Here is the problem. Many churches or denominations do not allow you to talk about this experience. They consider it a sin to struggle, to question, to doubt. They do not know that doubt is the leading edge of faith and that it is always important to find Christ in wonderful new ways. It is important to recognize that this desert experience will occur with regularity as you grow in faith.

In the past I had the experience of working as minister of education in a 2,000-member church. The senior pastor did something I had never seen a senior pastor—or any other pastor—do, for that matter. He held a Sunday school class each Sunday morning called "Doubters Anonymous." A place where persons who were in desert time could come, find support, share their experiences, and have a community of people to walk them through the experience. It kept many people from leaving the church because of their guilt for even having doubts.

Desert times are a stage of spiritual growth. So when you find yourself besieged by this profound stage, just stop for a moment and contemplate the depth of your experience. Please do not avoid it. Engage it as deeply as you can. There you will find God. There the spirit of the one who loves you deeply will come and abide with you because God is always there; you just happened to wake up in a fresh way to God's presence.

Additional Disciplines for Christian Living

There are many different disciplines that can help you on your spiritual journey. I list a series of them below.

- Scripture Reading: The reading of the Scriptures on a regular basis is essential for understanding how God has been with God's people throughout history. It is an endless resource of learning. The spiritually intelligent person is well informed of Jesus' teachings and his journey among us. But most important is the grounding of your faith in understanding how God continually communicates with us.
- Prayer: The daily practice of prayer, in all of its many forms, keeps you close to God, provides resources for every event of life, and brings meaning and hope to all that you do. In this book we discuss many ways of praying.
- Worship: Worship is not just an event that takes place on Sunday morning. It is also an attitude of the spiritually intelligent Christian. Worship is your approach to all of life. Worship's major feature is that of adoration, love, reverence, respect, and devotion. You may want to recall Brother Lawrence's approach when he says that there is no difference when he is working in the kitchen or when he is taking Communion. All is worship. It is a mind-set of how you

think, solve problems, work with others, and serve the world.

- Scripture Contemplation: This meditation process allows you to take a particular passage of Scripture and meditate on it. Meditation is when you consider the meaning of the text by reading it slowly and picking out particular words that resonate with you. What does this text have to say to you today? Look at each aspect of the text. Take the text apart and read it in small segments. If there are people in the text, who are they and how do you relate to them?

The following is one of the most familiar texts from the Scriptures: the good Samaritan story. You most likely learned it in Sunday school. I want to do something with this text that you probably have never done in your life.

First, list the characters in the story that Jesus tells. Don't include the donkey.

Following is the text of the story. How well did you do before reading it?

> Jesus replied, "A man was going down from Jerusalem to Jericho, and fell into the hands of robbers, who stripped him, beat him, and went away, leaving him half dead. Now by chance a priest was going down that road; and when he saw him, he passed by on the other side. So likewise a Levite, when he came to the place and saw him, passed by on the other side. But a Samaritan while traveling came near him; and when he saw him, he was moved with pity. He went to him and bandaged his wounds, having poured oil and wine on them. Then he put him on his own animal, brought him to an inn, and took care of him. The next day he took out two denarii, gave them to the innkeeper, and said, 'Take care of him; and when I come back, I will repay you whatever more you spend.' Which of these three, do you think, was a neighbor to the man who fell into the hands of the robbers?" (Luke 10:30-36)

Keep in mind the six characters in the story: the person who was robbed, the robber(s), the Priest, the Levite, the Samaritan, and the innkeeper. Usually we only consider the behavior of the good Samaritan and how we are to be like that. But meditate on the following: the people who have robbed you, hurt you, left you lying along the road of their lives, still wounded. You were the one being robbed.

Think of the people you have robbed, hurt, or greatly disappointed; they are lying along the road of your life. You were their robber.

Consider the people in your life whom you have avoided, and maybe still avoid. You even have a good rationale for avoiding them. Indeed, you are the Priest and the Levite.

Now list all of the people you have helped—you could make pages of them—you went out of your way to aid them. You were their good Samaritan.

Add a sixth person. List the names of people you have helped because someone referred them to you. You didn't wound them, but someone else asked you to help them because they were suffering from some injury or illness. You were their innkeeper.

Please note that the innkeeper is the person who ended up doing the long-term work. The good Samaritan paid the bill, but he left the robbed man in the hands of another to do the long-term healing.

When meditating on this text, you may come to realize that you are this whole story. You are not just the good Samaritan, you are also a person who has been robbed; you have also been a robber, an avoider (Priest/Levite), a good Samaritan, and an innkeeper. *You are the story.*

One of the meditation skills used in reading Scripture is to put yourself in the role of each person in the story. How are you like them?

Other areas for development can be added to this list, such as the following:

- Evangelism: The first spiritual intelligence reflects on this process. It simply asks how you share your faith story with another. How do you pass on the good news of Jesus Christ and the God who loves us?
- Service: Each person I interviewed could tell me stories of how he or she was a servant in the world. Some acts of service were simple; some were complex. Some persons cared for an elderly parent, others worked in a soup kitchen, while others called on shut-ins to listen to their stories. This spiritual discipline is the output of your life given to others.
- Stewardship: A steward is a person who manages another's property or financial affairs, or is one who administers anything as the agent of another or others. The Christian as steward takes on the responsibility of working with others so that they may achieve their goals. Often this is directed toward financial objectives and specifically when a stewardship committee develops a budget for a local church. To be the steward of the church funds requires that the person be highly trustworthy.
- It may be a much larger issue than just working with an individual or small group like a steward of the earth where you help conserve its resources. It can also mean to be a steward as a theological belief that humans are responsible for the world and should take care of it.

Another concept of stewardship falls into the area of spirituality. So for my purpose here, the steward is one who is responsible for the management of his spiritual life. But stewardship also incorporates how one manages others and one's relationship to others.

Jesus told many stories of stewards. I love the story (parable) that Jesus tells in these words from Luke 13:6-9:

> Then he told this parable: "A man had a fig tree planted in his vineyard; and he came looking for fruit on it and found none. So he said to the gardener, 'See here! For three years I have come looking for fruit on this fig tree, and still I find none. Cut it down! Why should it be wasting the soil?' He replied, 'Sir, let it alone for one more year, until I dig around it and put manure on it. If it bears fruit next year, well and good; but if not, you can cut it down.'"

There is an unusual role that the steward plays in this parable. The owner tells the steward of the vineyard to cut down the tree because it is unproductive. But the steward challenges the owner and tells him that he should wait one more year while he fertilizes it and then tells him that if it does not produce next year, "You can cut it down." He does not say, "Then I will cut it down." In fact, this is a parable where the steward acts on grace and my hunch is that each year he will say the same thing to the owner. So when we are not doing well, the steward says, "Let life fertilize him or her a little more so that he or she may produce the fruits of your love." So it is to be a steward. This leads us to a more specific application, that of integrating spiritual/biblical truth into your own life.

- Scripture Application: Scripture application is integrating the truth and meaning of a Scripture text into your own behavior. This is no small feat. I sat recently with an excellent adult group leader who told me that she was frustrated because after four years of work with her group, she saw very little evidence of any changes that these folks made in their lives as a result of the study of the Scriptures they had done together. She said that they all knew the subject well and could articulate the new information but, as she put it, "they never got it." Namely, they never incorporated the teachings of Jesus into their own lives. How do you apply the love of God into your own life? How does your faith show up and change as a result of your biblical insights? Having an insight, or an *ah ha* moment, is one thing; incorporating that new truth into behavior is another.

- Fasting: Fasting is one of the least-used spiritual disciplines. It requires that you know why you want to fast. If it is just for dieting—to lose weight—then you have to think again about your motivation. Yes, it may help with dieting; yes, it is the cleansing of the body, depending on the type of fasting you are doing. Fasting is not a quick way to lose weight. If you have questions about how appropriate a particular fast is for you, or if you have any concerns about how fasting will affect your health, please consult your physician.

At a spiritual level, fasting is about getting greater definition between your body and your soul. It engages a person with intense awareness that we are not just our bodies but much more.

Fasting gets you in touch with those who are dying of hunger. It makes you aware that many people do not have enough to eat. Your body soon tells you that it is hungry. There are many kinds of fasts. Some fasts allow juice only. Some people fast from a particular food, like chocolate, for a period of time.

A pastor friend of mine goes on a fruit juice fast every Lent. He drinks only specific kinds of juices that cleanse his body but still give him nourishment. He makes his own juice in a juice blender and, along with water, drinks about a quart a day. He generally loses about forty pounds during the Lenten season. I pushed him on why he did this. He responded that it is a type of calling for him. It makes him sensitive to others and wakes him up to God's presence. Some fasts extend from four to forty days. But again, a word of warning: if you want to fast for an extended period of time, please check with your physician. I once knew a young woman who wanted to grow deeper in her spiritual life by fasting. Given that she only weighed about 110 pounds, she wisely consulted her doctor. Her doctor said that with her body weight and amount of fat mass, a forty-day fast would kill her, even if she just abstained from solid food and drank liquids. He advised her to go no longer than three days, drink plenty of healthy juices, and take her multivitamins. Part of the point of the discipline of fasting is not to punish yourself but to learn your limitations and grow more dependent on God.

- Silence and Solitude: This spiritual discipline, next to the fast, is one of the more difficult for most people.

A story illustrates this point.

A pastor was seeking the help of a psychiatrist. During one of the sessions the psychiatrist told the pastor to go to his own office, to tell his secretary to hold all calls and visits, and to spend eight hours alone in his office—and do nothing. The next week, when the pastor returned for his scheduled visit, the psychiatrist asked him how the eight hours of silence had gone for him. The pastor said, "It was wonderful. I took my lunch with me. Sat in my reading chair, looked around my office, noticed books I had not completed, and pulled a few from the shelves and read them. I saw my music CDs and pulled out my favorite Beethoven symphony and listened to it while I read." The psychiatrist broke in and said, "No, no, no. I said I wanted you to spend eight hours in silence. No reading, no listening to music. Just be by yourself." The pastor is reported to have said, "That would drive me crazy."

The psychiatrist said, "You mean every Sunday you thrust on your congregation a man you can't stand?"

Being alone and quiet with yourself can be difficult because the moment you are quiet and alone a predictable experience takes place, such as a list of things you should be doing comes to your consciousness. It is important to get past that list and find what is behind it. I have discovered that high-level activity is the suppressant to personal pain. The reason we do not like to sit still is that we begin to become aware of our pain or anxiety. That very fact makes it important to be in silence so that we can deal with the deep inner pain that is within us.

The next discipline often accompanies the time of silence and solitude.

- Journaling: Several weeks ago I was looking through a box of books that I had moved from a previous home to our current one. There were pages from a journal that I had written some five years ago when I had prostate cancer. The reading brought back the memories, the anxiety, and the wonderful journey I have been on in the healing process. It was important for me to write my experience at the time, but I did not know the power of it until I reread it. Journaling is recording your thoughts and feelings for the sake of reflecting on your own journey. It gives you perspective and understanding.

Steve Pavlina is a coach and author and teaches journaling. He gives some good background to the journaling process. He says,

> Journaling is one of the easiest and most powerful ways to discover new truths. By getting your thoughts out of your head and putting them down in writing, you'll gain insights you'd otherwise miss.

> While some people use journaling merely to record their thoughts and experiences in a "Dear Diary" fashion, the real power of journaling lies in its ability to help you move beyond sequential thinking and examine your thoughts from a holistic, bird's-eye view. Use this tool to solve tricky problems, brainstorm new ideas, bring clarity to fuzzy situations, and evaluate progress toward your goals. Instead of a mere record-keeping tool, your journal can vastly accelerate your personal development if you devote it to that purpose.[4]

Here are three other powerful benefits of journaling:

- Some problems are very difficult to solve when you're stuck in an associative, first-person viewpoint. Only when you record the situation and then reexamine it from a third-person perspective does the solution become clear. Sometimes the solution is so obvious that you're shocked you didn't see it sooner.
- Gain clarity. A great time to turn to your journal is when you're just not clear about what to do. Should you quit your job to start your own business? Should you marry your current romantic partner? Are you on the right track financially? It's amazing how much clearer things become when you explore them in writing.
- Verify your progress. "It's wonderful to go back and re-read journal entries from years ago and see how much real progress has been made. When you're frustrated that your life doesn't seem to be working out as you'd like, go back and read something you wrote five years ago—it will totally change your perspective. This helps you in the present moment too by reminding you that you are in fact growing and changing, even when it feels like you're standing still."[5]

The next spiritual discipline is expanded at great length in

Step IV of the spiritual intelligences. I simply introduce it here for your awareness.

- Learning: Being a lifelong learner is essential to maintaining spiritual intelligence. It means that you are keeping your brain active and that you are engaged in experiencing life at its fullest.

I now want to continue in the prayer exercises.

Exercise IV: The Jesus Breath Prayer

This meditation and contemplation process is the simplest of prayers, yet one of the most profound.

Place your hands on your abdomen and become aware of the rhythm of your breathing. You will be able to feel your tummy move in and out as you breathe. Do this for fifteen to twenty seconds.

As you breathe out, say to yourself the name of Jesus, for about thirty seconds to a minute. Each time you breathe out say the name of Jesus again. If you do this for at least a minute, you will have repeated the name of Jesus about fifteen times.

The disciplined part of this prayer is to stay focused on the name of Jesus. If other thoughts start coming to your mind, kick them out and return to the name of Jesus. When you first start doing this prayer, you will be aware how difficult it is to say the name of Jesus for a minute without having extraneous thoughts come into your thinking. The discipline is to stay attentive to that name.

There is now a second step. After you have said the name of Jesus for at least a minute, stop and become still and silent. Now, listen for a response that may come to you. It may be a voice (word) that you hear, or some sensation in your body may get your attention, or a visual image of some kind may grab your awareness. Pay attention to it and speak to it. Again, you may get another response.

This will become the very early stages of a dialogue with Jesus/God. It may take many trials with the Jesus prayer before you become aware. On the other hand, I have had persons get an immediate response that surprised them and filled them with joy.

Try it. Put the book down and give it a try.

Advanced Jesus Prayer Strategy: In addition to the name of Jesus, you can now add a phrase, such as "thank you, Jesus," "Jesus, help," "Jesus, I bring you [name someone]," "Jesus forgive me," and so on. Again, the processes are the same in the breathing rhythm and repeating the phrase five to ten times—then remaining silent for some kind of response.

Exercise V: Engaging in Silent, Wordless Meditation

There are two ways to accomplish silent, wordless meditation:

1. The first way is a mediation style called the apophatic or negative (negative way), which is the imageless prayer. It is the process of emptying oneself of thoughts, feelings, and sensations. If this is the first time you have been introduced to the apophatic prayer, you may find this difficult or confusing to do. I did and often still do. It takes considerable practice but generates a great awareness of God's presence because there is nothing that is getting in the way. It is akin to centering prayer where one focuses on one word or phrase and deletes everything else so that God can come and speak to you without distraction. I will spend time on centering prayer at the end of this series of exercises.

A useful definition for apophatic prayer is that it refers to prayer without images. Here you simply call to mind that God's loving presence saturates all things, so you simply rest in a kind of general attentiveness to God, open to receiving whatever God wants to give. You come to know God as the ground of your own being and the presence at the heart of all things. No words can express this, and so apophatic prayer emphasizes loving silence and "unknowing" as distinctive features.

Dr. Frederick G. McLeod teaches apophatic and kataphatic prayer (more on kataphatic prayer in a moment) at St. Louis University. Dr. McLeod refers to his book *The Cloud of Unknowing*, which is a masterpiece whose influence is still widely felt in our own day. It provides a clear, concise, and convincing statement on what is "apophatic" prayer and how one can enter into it. For those who sense the need for a deeper experience, he urges a kind of prayer where one learns to be at home in a dark *cloud* beyond all thoughts and images.

To experience this type of prayer you must be ready (open) and prepared to simply direct your attention to God by using a word or short phrase. When a distraction comes along, turn it over to the care of God in prayer of petition, especially if it's a distraction you're concerned about. After turning it over, return to the special word or phrase you have chosen. Keep up this practice throughout your prayer time. Remember, prayer of petition is a form of prayer, and turning things over to the care of God is a form of surrender.

The apophatic prayer is often connected to the Jesus prayer I referred to earlier. Here is a specific strategy that can help you learn this form of prayer:

> Sit with your back straight, and chin slightly tucked in. Place your feet squarely on the floor and let your hands rest in your lap, palms up. Begin . . . and let your breathing become your "sacred word." . . . When you inhale, God is breathing life into you. . . . When you exhale, you are surrendering yourself to God. . . . Let your breathing be slow, prayerful, and deep, but don't try to force any particular pattern. If it becomes shallow, let it be that way . . . it will deepen . . . "reset" by the Spirit according to the Spirit's rhythm.[6]

2. The kataphatic prayer is very different. It uses all of your reason, will, imagination, feelings, and senses to first provoke your experiences, and then to channel these experiences toward specific goals. There is an interesting process to this that I have found useful.

Imagine that you are imprisoned in your own body. This can evoke strong feelings of helplessness and powerlessness. Now you are urged to nourish feelings of shame and confusion or any other strong feelings that may emerge. If all these feelings can be experienced, they create an effective mood and setting ideal for promoting a faith experience in which you have a heightened gratitude for God's love and forgiveness. It is in the polarity of such an experience that you come to wonder why you can have such feelings and still be loved by God. The prayer ends with a prayer of gratitude. It also urges you to ask three questions: What have I done? What am I doing? and What ought I to do? After exploring the first two questions, your mind will sort out the difference between what I should do and what I ought to do. This often leads to an ethical conversion where you change your behavior as a result of your reflection. When effectively implemented, "the ought to" becomes a "must."

Exercise VI: An Exercise in Stillness and Awareness

For many people, being still and quiet brings with it a sense of anxiety and unease. Our lives are full and running over with activities, such as taking our children to sports, going to church for myriad meetings, doing housework, or trimming the hedges in our gardens. We are driven by beliefs that if we are sitting still even for a moment, we are somehow inadequate. We even have sayings that perpetuate our chronic movement and work, such as "Idle hands are the devil's playground." So it is no wonder that this spiritual skill of prayer is so difficult for most of us. You may recall the illustration I used earlier, of the psychiatrist asking a pastor to be quiet for a day. This is no small matter of difficulty. Some background to this complexity may be useful.

My mother told me that if I would keep busy, my emotional problems would go away. There is some truth to this. Activity suppresses your emotional life. What is not true about my mother's statement is that the problem goes away—instead, it gets covered up, denied, buried. The result of this avoidance is that the problem becomes deprived of expression. You do not learn how to develop a vocabulary of your inner condition.

Sit quietly in a chair in a room devoid of noise. Sit there for five minutes. If you were to time yourself with a clock, you might believe that the clocked stopped. In this setting, time seems to slow down. As you sit there alone, you will begin to become aware of many thoughts, feelings, and sensations in your body making their way to consciousness. In this awareness, offer to God everything that emerges. What was hidden in you is now being revealed to you. God already knows what is there (God knows all your thoughts and feelings already). It is you who has to acknowledge these things. Offer everything that comes to your attention.

In addition, it is often helpful is to write down every thought and feeling that comes to you. It may be a part of your journaling. After you write it down, read it to yourself out loud. What are you saying to yourself and to God? The longer you sit quietly, the more experiences and thoughts will emerge. They may come very slowly or in a burst of insight. The discipline is to stick with that which emerges. There will be a strong tendency to get up "and do something." Try your best to not do that. As with all the exercises in this book, try to stick with it and experience it as fully as you can.

Practice these prayer skills as often as you can. You do not have to do them all at one time. Do one a day and then shift to another, or do one for a week or longer until you become very familiar with it, then add another. Be creative and create your own using these as models. These prayer forms are wonderfully renewing. Use them and become aware of how your prayer life will be enhanced.

STEP IV

Face Your Challenges: Finding God in the Spiritual Desert Times

In every person there is a spiritual strength which does not come from [within]. It can be refused or rejected but it is always there. It is never taken away. It is a well-spring of confident trust planted by the Spirit of the living God. Everything flows from this.

—*Brother Roger of Taize*[1]

Finding God in the Spiritual Desert Times

Stop dwelling on past events
and brooding over days gone by.
I am about to do something new;
this moment it will unfold.
Can you not perceive it?
Even through the wilderness I shall make a way,
and paths in the barren desert.
The wild beasts will do me honour,
the wolf and the desert-owl,
for I shall provide water in the wilderness
and rivers in the barren desert,
where my chosen people may drink,
this people I have formed for myself,
and they will proclaim my praises.

Isaiah 43:18-21 REB

The journey through the spiritual wilderness, frequently called desert times, is often frightening and yet wonderful. It comes sneaking up on us or arrives in a single moment. These spiritual transitions, these shifts of faith and understanding of God, are the next step of spiritual intelligence to explore.

My interviews revealed that each of those I listened to knew intensely about this part of her or his spiritual experience. This is where the ground of being seems like shifting sand. Yet these folks of faith learned that these times were an important part of their relationship with God.

It is important to note that these shifts and struggles occur approximately every five to seven years for the growing Christian. In some ways it is a decade phenomena. I hope your faith at the age of eighty is different from when you were eighteen.

In my training event on developing one's spiritual IQ, I introduce the language of desert time with an illustration of an e-mail I received from a former student. I have eliminated all references to the person, but left the rest of the information exactly as I received it. This e-mail was a cry for help in desert time. It represents the emotional condition and the struggle of a person who exhibits many of the attributes of the desert experience.

> Hi there:
>
> You always said to call, if needed. Well, I sure hope you meant it, because I sure need someone. When you realize a "life commandment" . . . how do you break its back? How do you take away its power? After a disappointment, or deep hurt, how do you remove the voices [and] the negative self-talk? . . . Is that all there is? . . . Then don't expect too much from life . . . and if you reach too high, you will only get disappointed . . . so, don't reach. I don't like that. . . . I always wanted to reach for the stars . . . and once did. But after many years of [having a]

> lack of confidence, I have stopped reaching . . . and now, [I] don't even know where to start. . . .
>
> You may not remember [me], but I did the Lab 2 workshop with you. I am feeling trapped in a ministry and with little fulfillment or reward, and almost nil appreciation (even worse. . . . I have just been roasted . . . on record, with little way to reply. I, like many others you have spoken with, was ready to resign . . . except I felt I had nowhere to go! Normally, I don't ask for such help. I just don't want to go under. . . . I don't want to merely survive . . . I want to live.
>
> Anyway, that all sounds a little too melodramatic . . . sadly. It is all true. So again, I would appreciate your reply. . . . Again, thanks for your assistance in the past.

This letter represents many of the issues of the desert time experience. It is often the feeling of being stuck, that life is a dead end, there is no place to go, that no one can help, thus the feeling of helplessness. It is the desire to live fully while feeling like you are dying inside and want to resign from the struggle.

It is a time when the beliefs that you have now seem inadequate for the journey you are on. The old beliefs that "don't expect too much" now create distress and extreme limitations on your life and future. Yet you have lived your life with those up to this time. There is a very deep agony and groaning inside.

You pray to God, and there does not seem to be any response. It is as if you are adrift, alone in the universe. It is, as William Bridges, an internationally recognized author and authority on managing change, told us in one of the training events he held for my company, what the *Peanuts* character Linus feels when his blanket is in the dryer. All the security has been taken away. You feel vulnerable and easily annoyed. You are out of alignment. This state of disorientation may be very mild, but it can also be very disconcerting.

This desert time is an in-between time. You are not what you were and you are not what you will be. Bridges refers to this state as a "neutral zone"—neither here nor there but in a time of gradual or rapid shifting.

Desert time refers to the time after the Hebrews were led out of Egyptian bondage by Moses. As they approached the Promised Land, spies were sent out to see what they would be up against. They needed to scope out the land so they could be prepared to face any dangers or obstacles. When the spies came back, they all reported that the land was full of giants. All, that is, except Caleb and Joshua, who gave a minority report suggesting that the people should proceed, take the land, and trust God. But the majority report swayed the people and none went into the Promised Land at that time. The consequence of their lack of faith was that the Hebrew people wandered in the wilderness for forty years (Numbers 13:25–14:25). They were not in Egypt, and they were not yet in the Promised Land.

This "middle state" has at its core a profound time for transformation. Yet this barrenness and despair is more often avoided because we typically run from that which wants to make us grow. But if we run from it, we miss a chance to become our best. Our lives become stagnant because we have avoided the deeper resources that are so needed at this time. The letter from the pastor tells of this condition. But then how do we maximize this time of desert experience?

Maybe a poetic metaphor can help you answer the question for yourself.

> That shattered lives can be made whole
> If handed to you willingly.[2]

Many people come to see me when they are in the desert. It is appropriate because there is help to be had in this wandering time.

Thrust into the Desert

What causes a person to be thrust into the desert? There are some predictors that you can pay attention to so that you may know why you are there.

A Series of Stressful Events (Emotional Clusters)

When life throws a sequence of events at you and your response is "Enough Lord, enough," you will be in touch with what I am talking about. Pay attention to how you are reacting to such a sequence. It evokes strong emotions and makes you feel vulnerable.

For twenty years I taught at Toronto School of Theology. I was part of the continuing education program and was invited to be a guest lecturer each May and November.

One evening a friend invited me to go with him to a lecture on the subject of cancer and storytelling. Since I have taught story listening for thirty years, I was more than intrigued, and we journeyed to the college auditorium. The professor that evening, whose name I have forgotten but whose teaching I will never forget, shared the emotional journey of a cancer patient. He talked about the collapse of an anticipated future—the hopes and dreams of a person and what happens to the person when he is told he has cancer.

I left that night with a deeper understanding of the desert. It is not just the cluster of events from the past that you bring to the desert, but the awareness of the loss of your dreams for the future. As the professor put it, "All of a sudden your future collapses into the present and there does not seem to be any outlook for your potential future life." It is as Jesus put it, "Let the day's own trouble be sufficient for the day" (Matthew 6:34 RSV).

There is only now, only the present. And for the desert experience that is sufficient. Many times we do not live in the present but are thinking about the past or the future. Desert time is "Now Time." You are forced to deal with the present condition and struggle and that is appropriate for this time in the spiritual journey.

I recently talked with a pastor who is in such a desert period. I asked her if she could see or think about where she might go as a result of her current setting. She didn't have a clue. That was quite all right. She has only been in the desert about three months, but on occasion I ask the question just to see if she is aware of anything in the possible future.

Experience the Desert

Meeting God in the desert only comes when you are willing to experience all that it brings. You cannot get "over" the desert or "around" the desert; you have to go through it. That means experience it. Feel it, talk to it, and see the fog and the uncertainty. *It is the time when you have to trust God in the not knowing.* If you have to know all the steps or the way out, you will not find a clear direction not at the beginning of the desert time anyway; but you will find a future and often a very clear purpose but only after you are there for awhile.

This is the time in your life when God is eminently present, but you do not recognize it. Why? Because you are about to wake up and discover God in a way you never thought possible. The God you wake up to is not the God who was there when you went comatose and forgot about God. Your relationship is going to change. It has the possibility of being more personal, more communicative, more life giving. Jesus said that he came "that [you] may have life, and have it abundantly." That is the hope that stirs in you while in the "not knowing" stage. The end result of these deserts is not just that it reworks your relationship with God but it also changes how you work and relate to others.

In the book *The Way of the Heart*, Henri J. M. Nouwen says:

> Solitude [of the desert] is not a private therapeutic place. Rather, it is the place of conversion, the place where the old self dies and the new self is born, the place where the emergence of the new man and the new woman occurs. . . . The wisdom of the desert is that the confrontation with our own frightening nothingness forces us to surrender ourselves totally and unconditionally to the Lord Jesus Christ. . . .
>
> Precisely because our secular milieu offers us so few spiritual disciplines, we have to develop our own. We have, indeed, to fashion our own desert where we can withdraw every day, shake off our compulsion, and dwell in the gently healing presence of our Lord. Without such a desert, we will lose our own soul while preaching the gospel to others. But with such a spiritual abode, we will become increasingly conformed to him in whose Name we minister. . . .
>
> If you would ask the Desert Fathers why solitude gives birth to compassion, they would say, "Because it makes us die to our neighbor." At first this answer seems quite disturbing to a modern mind. But when we give it a closer look, we can see that in order to be in service to another we have to die to them; that is, we have to give up measuring our meaning and value with the yardstick of others. To die to our neighbors means to stop judging them, to stop evaluating them, and thus to become free to be compassionate.[3]

The Structure of Resilience and How to Reclaim Your Personal Dream

God has built into us from early childhood the ability to bounce back from difficult times. This process is called resilience. We are often knocked off our equilibrium, but we have the ability to return to a stable state. The desert time is a time when we tap into our spiritual resilience and are in touch with the God who can right us again. These are resources that are rarely tapped except when we enter desert time. Often in this transition time of faith and life we focus on the pain, disruption, and confusion. However, there are strengths that are in all of us for the purpose of bouncing back, to the new faith and the new life that is ours if we can claim it.

When the loss of a dream takes place, and during the time of a set of clustered events, I urge you to write down those things that you have loved to do, those things that brought you great self-assurance and esteem. It is difficult to do this in close proximity to a cluster of events that really upset you. But you can do it within the months that follow. I call this mining the gold nuggets of your life. It is in this process that your resilience can help you find your way out of the desert.

Don't Hurry to Get Out

Don't be in too much of a hurry to get out of the desert. It has a lot to teach you and will give you inner strength. It is no accident that this desert period of life occurs on a regular basis, but once you have learned how to navigate this wilderness time, it becomes familiar ground, and it is not as frightening. Each desert period precedes a period of maturing, intelligence, and wisdom. It is how we grow up because it forces us to do problem solving and teaches us to resolve old feelings.

Desert time is a form of "spring cleaning" for the soul. Most of us store our experiences, particularly our pain, until the body, mind, and soul cannot contain them anymore and then—*bam!*—we experience intense problems in relationships, motivation, and our work life. God now provides a setting through which God can be present in this "get rid of this junk" time.

Now comes a warning to you. If you do not enter this time and clean house, so to speak, those issues will simply get submerged in your life and wait for another cluster of events to unearth them. Then you not only will have the current cluster of experiences to deal with, but the present situation will act like a low-pressure weather system and suck up the old experiences with it. Consequently, if you avoid the desert times in the first half of your life, you will pay a heavy price in the second half.

You do not need to worry that if you get resolution for the problems of the past ten years you will not have any in the future. The next decade will provide enough for you to deal with. If you lose a dream, you will have a chance to claim it again. You may remember that Christopher Reeve, who played the role of Superman, became a quadriplegic as a result of an injury he suffered in a fall from a horse. Most people would have given up, but he used the fall for his own inner development and even directed several films. We are resilient and the desert makes it so.

The desert time is a chance to slow down. It forces us to be still for a while and to listen to God, who is waiting to be known. Sometimes we are so frantically active that we miss the God we are trying to serve, even when serving in the church.

Thomas Kelly, in *A Testament of Devotion*, makes this point when he says:

> Some of the most active church leaders, well-known for their executive efficiency, people we have always admired, are shown, in the X-ray light of eternity, to be agitated, half-committed, wistful, self-placating seekers, to whom the poise and serenity of the Everlasting have never come. In some we regret a well-intentioned, but feverish over-busyness, not completely grounded in the depths of peace, and we wish they would not blur the beauty of their souls by fast motion. God wants your soul to grow, experience life's gifts, and has set in

> motion the desert experience so that you may have the opportunity to experience life in its fullness.[4]

God wants your soul to grow and experience life's gifts. Therefore, God sets in motion the desert experience so that you may have the opportunity to experience life in its fullness.

When you find yourself in this desert time, find a friend, pastor, or spiritual director. Most of all, don't run from the experience, but pay attention to all that it is bringing you, including all of its doubt and misery. Desert time, when worked on effectively, is merely transitory. It may last a few months or even a few years. To not engage it is to cause it to last much longer. Entering it will not kill you; although it may feel like it will. It is a time of metamorphism, a time of renewal and change. If you are in this stage as you read this book, put the book down for a moment, sit quietly, and be aware of the thoughts, feelings, and hopelessness you may be experiencing. It is OK; it will not last forever. It is transitory. The question to ask is: When this experience is over, what do you want in its place? That is your new hope. Go for it.

STEP V

Expand Your Understanding: Learn, Find Meaning in Your Life, and Be in Mission for Others

Each of the spiritually mature persons I spoke with made learning a key factor in his or her life. The expansion of the study factor was paramount for why each person became so spiritually astute. We will explore this in some depth. In addition, and this was a surprise to me, I saw how these persons developed the process of finding meaning—purpose, hope—in everyday experiences. The final section of this book is devoted to the ultimate outcome of spiritual intelligence. Now that I am spiritually mature, what do I do? Or, so what, I have spiritual intelligence? Last, we will look at these questions: Do I have to become spiritually intelligent before I can find what God has for me to do? And do I become spiritually intelligent as a result of searching for how I live out my life?

Learn throughout a Lifetime

The mature, spiritually intelligent person has the motivation and capacity to be committed to lifelong learning. Even after only a half dozen interviews, this concept popped out and clearly got my attention. What was interesting for me was that the range of learning was extensive. Regardless of the field in which the interviewees were engaged, they were able to bring their spirituality to it, and they could also bring their work or avocation to their spirituality.

The importance of learning and keeping the brain alive is one of the most important tasks of life. But staying motivated is not easy. We tend to get into ruts of thinking and make the assumption that what we already know is adequate for our lifetime. You certainly can live without expanding your mind or experiencing something new; but the long-term effect of such a lifestyle, however, is boredom and world-weariness.

There is an alternative, but it is even more difficult than the traditional form of learning. This option means that you reflect daily on your life, and review what you have done each day. This process will produce wisdom and understanding of self. But there is a dilemma with this process; it makes the assumption that you have the spiritual wisdom to make it a discipline for your life.

The following is a reflection guide for those who wish to learn a process of reflecting on daily experience.

Developing Spiritual Wisdom through Personal Reflection

The following series of activities, when processed effectively, will help you develop personal wisdom, both spiritual and practical. The difference between wisdom and education is that wisdom comes from learning from all of life's experiences, while being educated is the ability to learn from courses, books, teachers, and other sources of knowledge.

The Day-End Review

Begin by acknowledging your own personal inner wisdom, spiritual strengths, and love. This will enable you to center yourself as you explore your personal resources and capabilities. Acknowledge some of them as you begin this process:

1. *Run a movie of the day's activities.* At the end of the day, run a movie through your mind of the activities where God may have shown up for you, starting at the beginning of the day and proceeding throughout the day. Also list the events, conversations, and people you encountered throughout the day. With whom did you communicate today, either verbally or nonverbally?

Write the list here:

____

____

____

____

2. *Freeze-frame the movie at the "rough spots."* Stop the movie whenever you find places where you didn't like the response you got from others or where you didn't like your own behavior. This identifies the problem contexts.

3. *Identify resources to apply.* Ask "What worked?" What actions, feelings, ideas, responses, and ways of being worked well during the day? What other resources could I have used and applied from other contexts?

4. *Identify difficulties to address.* Ask two questions: "What did I do well and would want to do again, even better the next time?" and "What did not work?"

(a) How would I have liked to have affected others? (Spirit)

(b) What kind of a person did I want to be in this situation? (Identity)

(c) What did I deem as the most important concern in this situation? (Values)

(d) What did I feel certain of or want to feel certain of? (Beliefs)

(e) What was I able to do, or what would I have liked to be able to do? (Capabilities)

(f) What action(s) would I have liked to take or did I take? (Behaviors)

5. *Create the new reality*. Play the movie again, this time seeing yourself doing, feeling, being, acting, and so on, with all of the resources you imagined. Do so until *you generate a positive emotional response* to the new creative movie. To do this, keep recycling through the resource development step.

6. *Finish backtracking the day's movie*. Future pace (imagine you are doing these actions in the future), run an ecology check (how does the new thinking, feeling, acting fit into your new understanding of how you are with others and with God?), then enjoy the new experience.[1]

It has been my practice for many years to read a large variety of books. For many years, my wife has given me *Astronomy* magazine as a Christmas gift. It is one of my mind-bending activities to read most of them cover to cover. If you want to expand your mind, read about the universe. Did you know that there are as many neurons in your brain as there are stars in the Milky Way? A galaxy in your head.

In my life, I try to create at least one new training event every three years. It forces me to read, go to other training events, be with people who know a lot more than I do, and create new ways of learning. It is easier today to explore learning options than ever before. For example, the amount of subject material that is available on the Internet is phenomenal. Any subject is at your fingertips. Several months ago, just for fun, I searched the Internet for college courses online. You can earn a degree in almost any subject by sitting home and studying in your own place. Just type into your Internet's search engine "college courses online" and you will be overwhelmed with options.

Here is a list of areas of development that you may want to consider. It may open your world to other alternatives for study.

Arts
Health and Wellness
Culture
History
Literature
Philosophy
Religion
Writing
Information Technology
Languages
Life Sciences
Physical Sciences
Math
Social Sciences
Economics and Finance
Political Science and Law

These subjects may strike you as secular and not spiritual. My intention here is to make you aware of what it may take to keep your brain alive and well, and your knowledge expanding. You certainly can go to online seminaries and universities as well. Type in "Bible courses" and see what happens.

The church that I attend is currently starting an academy of religious studies so that all members of the congregation may take many different types of courses for a very nominal fee. Our objective is to have the most highly trained clergy and laity as possible. Your faith community can do that too.

There is an overriding question that may help you focus on looking toward expanding your life and serving God throughout your life. What kind of Christian do you want to become in your lifetime? What disciplines do you want to develop? What kind of relationship with God and other people do you want to experience during your many trips around the sun?

If you let this experience of life be random, with no intention, there will be little determination on your part for the kind of growth that will happen. On the other hand, if you consider this book with intentionality, read and reread these chapters, you will be able to be more deliberate in achieving the outcome you want. This requires that you become proactive with your life rather than passive or reactive. However, your ability to be reactive can be very useful. Sometimes, when a cluster of events hits you, it makes you reconsider the direction and meaning of your life.

As a result of an ego-deflating experience, my brain is healthier now than five years ago. I have been quite healthy throughout my many years. As a result, my wife and I considered purchasing a long-term nursing home policy, just in case we become ill and need long-term care. I had to have a physical to get the insurance. A nurse came to our home to spend about an hour asking me questions about my health. I knew I was in good shape so I had little anxiety about the process. The nurse and I sat on opposite ends of our three-cushion couch. She asked me questions and everything was going well. She then told me that she was going to give me a memory test (I had never had one before) and she held up a single page of paper with sixteen words in big print—two columns of eight. She asked me to memorize as many words as possible and at the end of the exam she would ask me to tell her how many words I could remember. I said, "OK," and she gave me about thirty seconds to memorize the words. We completed the test, and she then finished the rest of the exam. About an hour later she asked me to tell her the words. I struggled, and out of the sixteen words I could only remember three. She said, "OK" and made no other comment.

Several weeks later I received a notice that I had been rejected for the policy. All of the rest of my physical health had been perfect, but I was rejected because I had to remember at least six of the words on the list to be accepted. I was emotionally deflated. How could that have happened? But it did. Was I losing my memory? Was I getting dementia or Alzheimer's disease? This event left me profoundly concerned. I called my physician and told him of the event. He asked me to come in, saying, "I will give you another test." He did. I flunked it. Now I was really concerned and anxious. I thought, "What should I do?"

While all of this was going on I received an ad in the mail from an organization that talked about their research and program on brain development. The program claimed that it had significant research from the major universities of the world and that the program they offered could return your brain to the memory level you had ten years earlier.

I often question such ads but thought I would order their free demo and so made a call to their offices. When I received the demo, I was more than impressed by the way it worked and I called and ordered the whole program. It required that I participate in the process one hour a day for forty days. I did so. It was more than challenging but also a lot of fun. As I reached the halfway mark, I was aware that my forgetfulness was lessening, and that my creativity was greater. By the time I finished the forty days, I felt a new sense of wholeness and could not believe that these scientists from over fifty universities had developed such a marvelous process.

Some of you may know the writings of Dr. Daniel Goleman and his books on emotional intelligence. I discovered that he was on the board of directors and was the vice president of production of Posit Science. That alone gave me the confidence to order the DVD. When I completed my exercises, I called my doctor, made an appointment to see him, and asked him to give me another memory test. He did. I scored 100 percent. I walked out saying to myself that it is possible to keep the brain active. I tell this story simply to let you know that if you *are intentional* about keeping your mind alert and your brain developing, there are lots of ways to do this.[2]

It's Never Too Late

Whether by chance or by God's good timing, you may be an older person who is wondering how much spiritual maturity you can develop in your older years. Oh, I hope you are asking those kinds of questions. There is much hope, yes, much. I refer you to the last chapter of Kilian McDonnell's book *Swift Lord, You Are Not*. What a marvelous book of prose. But pay attention here: McDonnell was seventy-five when he *first* started writing poetry, and his best work was in his eighties. The last chapter talks about his experience as an older man trying to find some new gift that God had placed in him that had lain dormant for nearly six decades. He had published scholarly theological books and articles and thus had written theology for many years, when a friend told him to stop writing theology and start writing poetry. He did.

In that same chapter he talks about all the creative people who started much of their creativity in their seventies and eighties. After all, you now have a lifetime of experiences to bring to your understanding. For heaven's sake, and I do mean heaven, don't die before you die. Take all the moments of your life that have afforded you a time to reflect on the gifts that God has given you. Maybe now that the kids are long gone, and the grandchildren or great-grandchildren are around your knees, you may take a big breath and remember what you have always wanted to do and never did. Now during that big breath, imagine you are doing it. It does not have to be grand, but it could be.

This book is an expression of my experience on this planet and comes not only from the input of others but also from my own spiritual experience. Just imagine that if I have had at least three experiences a day, I will have had over 86,000 experiences in my lifetime. This accumulation of days is a gift that should not be misrepresented in your life. The outpouring of your life should come from that which has been poured into you. Don't squander that which you have so preciously accumulated through your experience. God has enriched you every day. The issue, of course, is what you have done with those experiences.

Do you remember the list of spiritual disciplines that I referred to earlier in this book? Things like Scripture reading, prayer, worship, scriptural meditation, evangelism, service, and stewardship. If you are older, you may have six, seven, eight, or even nine decades of encounter with God to enrich you and bring you to a time of wholeness in soul. This often is a time of silence and solitude. Just turn off the TV and notice what happens to you.

Maybe a prose response will come to you like it did to McDonnell. Maybe you will find something very deep inside that begins to ask questions:

Marcia from Poland

At four she wonders
Where God lives
on Mondays,
and if it's cold
and snows in heaven?
Who cooks
God's steaks,
Mops the floor,

Makes the bed?
Does God have a belly-button,
Eat turnips
Does God bite?[3]

Maybe you should write a poem as a result of an encounter with a child, maybe write a song, maybe draw a picture, and maybe make a photo album of yourself and each friend you have, to be remembered by those who have loved you. What would you have to do now to start or keep the journey of your mind alive? It is the greatest gift God has given you. Please do not squander it; do everything possible to not die before you die. Use your mind, grow it, and develop it as long as you live. Exercise, meet with your favorite friends, travel if you can, and pray with all your heart. It is healthy for your heart and your mind.

Capacity to Find Meaning in All Life

Remember that the steps to mature spiritual intelligence do not occur in any particular sequence. They could, in fact, be put on a wheel with each spoke running into the center, where the IQ is developed. They are, however, highly connected and interactive.

There was no doubt in my mind that spiritually intelligent persons have the ability to seek out the meaning of their life experiences. It is that quality that makes all of the other intelligences useful and productive. For example, if desert time had no meaning for these people, they would not have been able to sustain the rigor and tenacity to go through such a wilderness and reshape their beliefs. It was, in fact, the meaning of such an adventure that allowed them to grow through the experience. If sharing their faith with another did not have intrinsic meaning, they would not have continued distributing the good news of Jesus to those they met. So it is with knowing your story, praying deeply, simplifying your desires, and facing your challenges.

The Exploration for Meaning

All of us have the need to find meaning in what we are doing. We tend to move away from or ignore those events in our lives that are meaningless, empty, and hollow. So what is this process and how is it that meaning is so important?

Viktor Frankl is by far the most authoritative person in the field of meaning. His experience in a German concentration camp gave him the experience of discovering meaning in the worst of all conditions. If you wish to explore his teachings, simply go to your local bookstore or find him on the Web. His best-known book is *Man's Search for Meaning.*

The most powerful of all of his concepts is the idea that you can take away my clothes, you can try to starve me, you can beat me with a rod, you can threaten to kill me. But there is one thing you cannot do to me; you cannot take away my ability to choose how I will interpret my experience.

This may seem controversial, but all events in your life are neutral. They only mean what you bring to them. That is why when an event occurs there are many interpretations of it. So the interpretation you bring is what it becomes. Take several events that happened to Jesus and note the different interpretations that were given to them. In chapter 27 of Matthew we have this statement:

> Next day, that is, after the day of Preparation, the chief priests and the Pharisees gathered before Pilate and said, "Sir, we remember how that imposter said, while he was still alive, 'After three days I will rise again.' Therefore order the

> sepulchre to be made secure until the third day, lest his disciples go and steal him away, and tell the people, 'He has risen from the dead,' and the last fraud would be worse than the first." Pilate said to them, "You have a guard of soldiers; go, make it as secure as you can." So they went and made the sepulchre secure by sealing the stone. (Matthew 27:62-66 RSV)

The meaning of this event through the eyes of the religious people of the time (priests and Pharisees) is different from what we now believe or even what the disciples believed after they saw Jesus again. The events change meaning. So for each person, the event became what he brought to it from his own experience.

This is not to say that traumatic events can be trivialized, but the person who experiences a trauma does have options for interpretation. I know of a woman who was raped for four hours by a man who got into her house. I have talked with her many times about the event. Its initial shock was severe. But with help, the woman moved from being emotionally distraught to a person who became a counselor for other women who had been raped. She chose to take the event and turn it into helping others. She could have done many other things as a result of the incident. She could have seen it as the end of her life or destroyed herself with drugs or alcohol. She could have avoided all men, but instead she found a loving person to whom she has been married for many years and with whom she has had several children. The event does not have to dictate the outcome. The person to whom it happens makes that determination.

There is also a wide range of interpretation, even among Christians who hold many of the same beliefs. I have worked with over forty different denominations and each brings its own interpretation and meaning to the Christian story. What happens in that process is that each of us comes to believe that the meaning we each draw from the event equals the truth. And some believe that if you don't draw the same meaning that they do then there is something wrong with you. Consequently, groups of people band together who have something of the same meaning (interpretation). But no two people see everything alike and no two people believe exactly the same things, just as no two eyewitnesses tell the same story or hold exactly the same truth.

The key to finding meaning is to bring the most life-giving meaning to any event. Meanings can change as a result of your context and your interpersonal relationships; and thus the meaning you started with is not the one with which you ended.

There is an old Chinese story that makes this point:

> A Chinese farmer was known to have more money than the rest of the farmers because he had a horse. The horse allowed him to plow more fields and take his crops to more distant communities. He was a very generous man and shared his wealth with those in the community who needed help.
>
> One morning the farmer awoke and discovered that the corral gate had been left open and that his horse had run away. Members of his community found out about the event and came to him to share their condolences, saying, "We are sorry to hear that your horse has run away. Now you will have less money." The farmer responded with only one word: "Maybe."
>
> Several days later his horse returned with two wild stallions. Again the community heard about this event and returned to him and said, "You are lucky. Now you will have three horses and you will be wealthier than ever." The farmer simply said, "Maybe."
>
> The following day, the farmer's twenty-year-old son, in an attempt to ride one of the wild stallions, was thrown from the horse and broke his leg. After the news of the fall found its way to the community, people came to the farmer's farm to share how sorry they were that his son had broken his leg and how discouraging that must have been for the farmer. Again, the farmer said, "Maybe," because a week later the army conscription officers came through the community taking away their twenty-year-old sons to join the army, but they did not take his son because he had a broken leg. Again his friends returned

and said how fortunate he was to not have his son go to the army where he might be killed. The farmer said, "Maybe."

This story is called a reframing story. The meaning of each event changes in the light of another event. Reframing gets its name from the fact that when you put a different frame around a picture, the picture looks different.

We, as Christians, are the greatest reframers in history. We took an event that was an object of derision to the world, namely the cross, and with God's grace, turned it into the grace and love of God. That's changing the meaning of an event.

The work of being spiritually intelligent is, at least in part, the ability to draw significant meaning from the events of life that bring one purpose and understanding. The work of being spiritually intelligent is one of the most difficult tasks of spirituality. During the training event in which I teach persons spiritual intelligence, I ask people to list an event and its possible meanings. For example, let's say you get laid off or fired from your job. How do you interpret that event? What is its meaning? Here is a list of possibilities:

- They are lousy employers.
- I was not good enough for the job.
- They are more concerned about money than about people.
- They kept people who were not nearly as competent as I was.
- I'm a loser anyway.
- I wanted a different job anyway; this will give me the chance to look.
- Maybe now I can go back to school and get a better job.
- At least they gave me two weeks' notice.
- I'll never find another job.

Which one of these is the correct answer? Is there a correct answer? What the person brings is what the event becomes, right?

Just for fun, let's make this process a bit more complex. There are many different ways in which to decode—(interpret) meaning of an event. Here are a couple.

1. Linguistic meaning is communicated through the use of spoken words. This becomes very complex because what you understand the person to mean may in many ways not be what the person intended. Part of this is not just the words themselves but the tone that accompanies them.

I am currently working with a young pastor who has had a great deal of difficulty managing conflict in her church. Any word of criticism, even if constructive, she decodes as being *against* her. This makes her ability to receive feedback almost impossible. She reads (interprets) the person's behavior as meaning that she or he does not like her and that means for her that she is inadequate. So the meaning is drawn from not only the input she gets but also mostly from how she decodes it. The event becomes her interpretation.

2. Nonlinguistic or extralinguistic meaning is intentional communication without the use of verbal language. If linguistic meaning is complex, this type of meaning is even more difficult to obtain. What meanings can you draw from another person's behavior, that is, the movements and gestures a person uses without saying a word?

Several years ago, a church executive whom I trained in advanced listening and caring skills had the chance to take my materials and translate them into the Coptic Egyptian language so he could teach Christians in Cairo. Upon his return to the United States, I had a chance to debrief his experience with him. Out of the many things he experienced, he told me a rather funny story, saying that if I ever went to Egypt to do training, I would have to change one of my behaviors or I would be in trouble.

Frequently, in our culture, if you want to say something is good or "right on the ball," you will take your hand and make an *o* with your thumb and first finger and say, "Right on the ball," meaning "good work," "I liked it," and so on. My friend told me that if I did that in Egypt, I would be very offensive because the o equaled the back end of a camel. What I would mean by the gesture and what Egyptians would draw from it would be opposite. This just means that the message you send is not always the one that is received. It should be noted that language across the years changes and bring a different meaning. For example, every time the word *passion* is used in the New Testament, its meaning is radically different from how we use the word today. Following are a few verses that express how *passion* is used:

Romans 1:26 (NASB): "For this reason God gave them over to degrading passions."

1 Corinthians 7:9 (NASB): ". . . for it is better to marry than to burn with passion."

Colossians 3:5: "Put to death, therefore, whatever in you is earthly: fornication, impurity, passion, evil desire."

1 Thessalonians 4:3-5: "For this is the will of God, . . . that each one of you know how to control your own body in holiness and honor, not with lustful passion, like the Gentiles who do not know God."

There has been a dramatic shift of meaning of a word from the times of the New Testament to our time. More often than not, when we use the word *passion*, we think of it in positive, not negative terms. The New Testament's orientation is from the Greek word *pathos*, from which we get the word *pathology*—an emotional illness or sickness. Today we think of *passion* with quite an opposite interpretation.

Occasionally, I even get into trouble in different cultures with the words I use. Recently, I did a weeklong training event in Newfoundland. In one of my opening presentations I used the word *stupid.* I occasionally use that word in a light, fun context. Immediately after I had used that word in my first presentation, the province executive of the denomination, whom I greatly respect, pulled me aside and asked that I not use that word because it was offensive in that culture. I changed my behavior. Clearly, what I meant by the word and what they understood that same word to mean were different.

Meaning as Values or a Value System

Some of the great Greek philosophers saw values as guides to excellence in thinking and action. In this context, values are standards that we strive to achieve and they are practical habits that enable us, as individuals, to live, be successful, and achieve happiness. The meaning of values, however, represents one of the most consistent forms of conflict among people, particularly in the church. What one member values may be radically different from what another sees. So even the standards and norms within a group may be very different from one another.

In our church we have two worship services. One is rather traditional in structure while the other is quite a different setting. One has a choir; the other has a praise band. The people who go to each of these services see the role of worship in different ways. What one values in worship is clearly evident in the different styles of worship. People who once in a while shift to the other service may walk away and say, "I didn't find anything meaningful in that worship service." What is interesting is that this comment is said when people from either service go to the other. It's all in what you bring to the event, right?

Spiritual Intelligence and Meaning

So what is so special about the spiritually intelligent person and her assessment of meaning? The number one response from these people were questions such as "How is God in this event?" and "How does God show up in this experience?" These people always look for God. God becomes the key to their interpretation of meaning. There is the belief that God is in all events. For them, there is no episode of life without the presence of God. This becomes the basis for the meaning of each experience of daily existence.

Remember Brother Lawrence from a previous chapter? God's presence was even in the kitchen with the pots and pans. This spiritual awareness determines the interpretation of the event and solidifies its meaning. For Christians the interpretation involves an understanding of the life, death, and resurrection of Jesus.

For people who have achieved spiritual maturity, God is present in both the gift and the flaw—in life and in death, in sickness and in health, in pain and in joy. It is much more important for them to ask, "What does this mean?" than to ask, "Why did this happen?" We may never know why something happens, but we can always seek to find its meaning.

I wish life were as simple as that which I just presented; and that the meaning of life could be discovered easily, but some things in life are vague and uncertain.

There is little in life that is only black and white or just a choice between this and that. Most of the time, life is full of ambiguity. And often there is no clear choice between this or that. It is usually difficult to exactly determine the meaning of what has happened or what is said. And sometimes our language does not help, because language itself presents many paradoxes.

In philosophy and logic, the liar paradox encompasses paradoxical statements such as "I am lying now" and "This statement is false."

And related to it (there are many of these) is Epimenides' paradox: "A Cretan says, 'All Cretans are liars.'" Finding meaning in paradoxes is often confusing and uncertain. But this meaning does illustrate the complexities of living and making decisions.

Here is an illustration modeled after the Ship of Theseus paradox. This paradox raises the question of whether an object that has had all its component parts replaced remains fundamentally the same object.

This paradox can also apply to groups and churches, because it seems that you can replace any member of the congregation and it will still basically be the same congregation. You can replace all members, one at a time, and you will still be left with the same congregation. But if you can take all of those people who were replaced and bring them together, do you still have the same congregation you started with?

The point is that there are limits to logic and our ability to make rational choices. Meaning cannot always be clear or easy. Sometimes the best we can do is be willing to be confused.

A final way you can consider the elements of meaning is to write down a number of events that have happened to you. Jot a few down in the left column. In the column to the right, list all the meanings you could draw from the events listed on the left. See the following chart.

Name several events.	Describe one or more meanings that you could draw from each event. Which meaning best serves you and God?

The spiritually intelligent person focuses on the meaning that most fosters her life, brings hope, and provides a viable future. This is not easy and it will likely take you a lifetime to master the act of finding a productive meaning for all that you do.

Whom Shall I Serve?

This question, asked by spiritually intelligent people, is the culmination of that which I have discussed in this book. Once you have developed some or all of the intelligences, you are presented with what I call the Lucy Syndrome. In the *Peanuts* comic strip there is a familiar scene of Lucy behind a roadside psychiatric booth that looks a lot like a lemonade stand. From time to time, Charlie Brown pays his nickel to earnestly seek Lucy's professional advice. After he pours out his heart, Lucy inevitably gives Charlie Brown a lecture. When she is finished, Charlie says, "Now that I know that, what do I do?" So now that you have read this book and learned about the steps to mature spiritual intelligence, you might ask, "Now, what do I actually do?" or "Spiritual intelligence, so what?"

The questions are: How do you put your spiritual intelligence into practice? How does it show up in your life? What difference does it make to you for your daily living? Would anyone know you are a spiritually intelligent Christian by observing your behavior?

Consider the following concepts. There are two things that should be intrinsically linked together: your spiritual intelligence and your passion. Your passion represents your excitement and enthusiasm about your life and, in particular, what you want to do. It may be your career, your volunteerism at church or other service agency, playing in the praise band, singing in your local church choir, or teaching a Bible course. Your passion may be for life itself because you awaken every morning wanting to do what you love to do. Passion is your deepest driver, that which motivates you to do your best in whatever you are doing. When that does not happen and passion is missing, you will get a very different result.

You know you are passionless when everything seems to be drudgery or merely routine. If you attend a passionless church, the worship services are "death warmed over"; there is no energy in the singing, no fervor in the preaching, and no vigor among the people. When passion is present among the people, you can feel it. It lifts you up, brings you joy and hope. It fills the room with positive energy because each person there is fully committed to the love of God and to finding God there. In passionate churches, each member either has his own specific ministry or is searching for one. The air is full of expectancy. People are excited about their spiritual life and interested in cultivating spirituality in others, even if it is hard work—and it is.

Michael Slaughter, who is the senior pastor of Ginghamsburg United Methodist Church in Tipp City, Ohio, has mastered the passion process. I have had the privilege of twice being a consultant to his marvelous congregation. He has taken the church from ninety members to more than four thousand. He has a general rule that he quoted me: "You are not a member of this church until you can tell me/us what your passion for ministry is." As he put it, "I do not want to have a passionless church. If you don't have a passion for Christ, we will help you find one."

Testing Your Motivation and Passion

Over the last several years I have been using a little process to help people sort out their motivation and passion for their job or volunteer work. I have found it to work well, and it gets people in an organization to talk about what motivates them to do their best work. I got the idea from the motivational "sort" concept in the neuro-sort training with Dr. Gene Rooney. A neuro-sort is the process by which the brain, your neurology, sorts your world by accepting something as reality. It can also distort it enough to accept it or delete it. Let me explain the process, its accompanying language, and the settings in which you may want to use it.

Let's assume for a moment that you want to find the key motivators and passions for some of the people you work with or for those in your organization who are volunteers. Use the following survey with your group. Discuss the results as a group. These questions and comments allow a person to sort through her motivational criteria. If you are asking people to work only at levels three or four (please see below), you will get precious little work from them. They will resist or sabotage and basically be unproductive. In motivating your people, find out what levels 1 and 2 are for them and then respond to those levels. This process can be used at staff meetings, church board retreats, job interviews, work task forces, ongoing committees, in encounters with employees, or even with your spouse. Let me hear from you as to how you have used these suggestions.

This motivation assessment is valuable as a research tool for any size group or for individual use. Print the four statements that follow on page 115 and hand them out. Then record your findings. When you gather your findings, note levels 1 and 2. These are the most positive motivational parts of the person's life. They also represent the person's strongest passion. That is, those things that generate energy and purpose for the person's life. Levels 3 and 4 may mark potential passion, but for most people they are levels of resistance and the person does not show much energy for them. Level 3, and particularly 4, creates resistance either because a person has had some negative experience or is completely untrained in the areas required.

If the church wanted you to become a pilot in a plane that carried supplies to starving children in Africa, you might like the idea and have some passion for the task, but if you have never sat in the cockpit of a plane, you would most likely say no to that request.

What is marvelous about this process is that someone may be at levels 3 and 4 but find a calling in a different area. This person may then go and become trained to fulfill those tasks in that different area and move from level 4 to level 1. Low passion at one time in your life may become a high passion later on. It can go the other way as well. You may have a wonderful passion that is driving your life, until a series of events takes place that makes it difficult to keep that passion. You then have to shift it to one that may be lying latent in your life.

Motivation/Passion Criteria

1. What is it that you do really well—your highest level of skill and expertise? This should be something you are self-motivated to do because it brings you great satisfaction, and when you do it you know you are doing a good job. (This level is the highest form of self-motivation; you do not have to be asked to do it, you just do it.) It is your greatest passion.

2. What is it that you do well, but only if you are asked? Identify something you do with excellence because it is a part of your expertise and passion, but that you are not likely to be self-motivated to do. You have a passion for it, but you act on it only when invited.

3. What is it that you resist doing because you believe you do not do it well and you do not particularly like doing it? At this level, you will do this task if you are pushed or required to (i.e., it is part of your job description), but typically it does not bring you satisfaction, and you have little passion for it.

4. What one thing do you refuse to do because you are not good at it, and doing it makes you very uncomfortable, or maybe even embarrassed? You are not skilled in it and you have little or no passion for it. When asked you usually say no.

Extending Your Passion to Others

The persons I interviewed found ways of extending their witness and passion to a large variety of people. One of the most profound examples I know is a friend and colleague who is currently the president of the World Choir Games. Hugh Ballou is from Virginia and is an excellent musician and choral conductor. Because he wanted to extend his choral conducting passion to a wider group of people, he began to invite choirs from around the world to a world-class competition in the grandest cities on our planet. He had some four hundred choirs come together in Europe from many countries in the world. They performed more than three thousand concerts in the area and then on a final evening, those choirs came together, and Ballou conducted the concert of some ten thousand singers. He expanded his talents, beyond what he ever thought possible, to achieve a dream driven by his passion to open the choral doors of the world. All you have to do is be in his presence for ten minutes to know the energy and passion of this man.

Extending your passion does not have to go to the world level; it just has to go past where you are. Push the edge and expand your world. Most of all, get out of the ruts of your everyday world. Look at the possibilities for where your passion can take you. Find other people with the same passion and brainstorm how your worlds can expand.

I am a dreamer but also a realist. I know that it can be difficult to expand our worldview and share our witness with others. We become so comfortable in our small worlds that we begin to believe that what we see and know is all there is. Don't believe that. Your soul longs for and needs a large variety of experiences in order to grow.

Jesus never traveled more than fifty miles from the place of his birth. He expanded his world by the great number of *different* people he ministered to within that fifty-mile range. That is another way of expanding yourself and your world. How many different kinds of people are in your area? How many different needs are there for you to explore?

While working with many people is one method, another is to work with only one person who is very different from you. For years, Henri Nouwen took care of an extremely disabled man. Nouwen had to feed him, wash him, and diaper him. Nouwen devoted himself to care for this other person because it pushed his own soul to extend itself beyond his own personal boundaries. The spiritually intelligent person seeks to find those places in his or her life that will give the soul a chance to get out of itself and move toward the needs of others.

To expand your spirituality, there is a specific model that can be useful.

Hugh Ballou's S.M.A.R.T. Model

Hugh Ballou has developed a model in which you can get your thoughts and life organized so that you can accomplish your dreams. It can provide a way of thinking so that you can stay focused on your outcome. I like the model because it is simple and practical.

S = Specific

Choose some specific thing that you would like to do (that you are passionate about) and identify some *specific* thing, project, task, or way of being that you want to accomplish. Make it practical and something that you believe you *can* accomplish. Then, identify particular persons who might help you get this accomplished.

M = Measurable

To keep this realistic, you must be able to measure your progress along the way. That keeps your dream within bounds and does not let it get so ethereal that it can never be achieved. In business, we call this process "benchmarking." One way to benchmark is to map out the strengths, weaknesses, opportunities, and threats (commonly called SWOT Analysis). This will help you compare what you are dreaming about with others who have done the same or something similar. If you wish to push your edges, talk with others who have done the same.

Measuring your passion can be a bit daunting. Jan, the person I spoke about in the introduction, was able to do this by doing a very specific bit of planning. She wanted to get a PhD in counseling. It meant a great deal of sacrifice for her, but the passion was so strong that she paid the price. What she did was to break down the dream/passion into very small chunks. She worked in ninety-day segments, measured her success within those segments, and soon found that her dream had a real chance of becoming a reality. Because she is a person skilled in meditation, she was able to see herself going through each stage until she succeeded.

A = Accountable

Most of our personal mission expansion occurs without this step. If you set out to explore the possibility of challenging your own status quo, you need to tell someone else what you are planning and have this person help hold you accountable for that plan. Today, the role of that person is often referred to as a coach. This can be a person who simply meets with you on a regular basis to see how you are progressing with your plans, and provides support and encouragement, or it can be a trained or professional coach who will help keep your feet to the fire so that you are able to solve all of the problems that will arise along the way.

If you are choosing to expand your own spiritual intelligence, then a spiritual director would be the best person to have serve as your coach. A spiritual director is a person who is trained to help you find and create the best relationship with God possible during your lifetime. As a coach and spiritual director, I have helped many people achieve their spiritual goals. Working with persons who are highly motivated to expand and develop their relationship with God and others is one of the most rewarding experiences anyone can have.

One goal of a spiritual director is to keep the person accountable in accomplishing the things she has set out to do. It is my experience that when a person says, "This is what I want to accomplish," she will set up every resistance possible to make sure it does not take place. That may surprise you, but it is true. When you listen to a person share her dream, say, "That's great. When you are going to do it?" And she often will tell you about all the things she has to do first before she can address it. That is why change is difficult and why it is often very difficult to do alone.

R = Realistic

Realism implies that at this time and in this place, this goal, dream, and passion of yours has some degree of likelihood of becoming a reality. In the field of neuro-sorts there are three primary kinds of sorters. Being a Realist is one of them, with the other two being Dreamer and Critic. The Realist is a person who thinks in logical sequences. He is an excellent planner; that is his gift. He intuitively understands a strategic plan and prefers to be guided by one. So in setting out how to expand your world to others, it is often helpful to have a plan. The plan needs to be Specific and Measurable, and you must be held Accountable for it. If you are not a realist, you might want to find one to help hold you accountable or to help shape your plan.

There is an approach that is taken both by project planners and those who work with a process called the Well-Formed Outcome, in which you start the planning with the end results and then work backward. When your dream of extending yourself to others is in place, what will it look like? When you are there, how will you know? Then you move backward in the plan to identify all that has to take place to get there. It is a very effective way of thinking and planning.

T = Timing

The timing of any dream for extending yourself to others is crucial to its success. So simply ask yourself: is this the right time to do this? By looking at the end result, is there anything in the ending that would tell you this is the time to do this?

There is a crucial dimension that will let you know that God is working in the plan with you. The dimension is that of using your connections. You know the plan is viable when the people you are with react positively to your idea, support your plan, and bring encouragement. Every expansion of your life brings consequences, and it is important to have a support group to help you do it. Let me give you an example.

Many years ago I was invited to be a trainer at a large conference in Hershey, Pennsylvania. The conference was sponsored by an international organization called Lifeline, with headquarters in Sydney. Here are the connections made before, during, and after the event:

- A pastor came to a training event that I led. The event was sponsored by his denomination.

- The pastor's wife became the international conference coordinator. In talking with her husband about whom to invite, he suggested me. She called me and my calendar was open for the three-day event (Timing).
- At the conference people from Brisbane took my workshop.
- On the way back to Australia, those who attended my workshop shared audiotapes made at the convention with the Brisbane executive.
- The Brisbane executive called me to see if I would train for his Lifeline organization. I said yes. We set the dates and place.
- Three months before the event, the Brisbane executive had a heart attack, and he called me and canceled the event. I thought that would end the connection. But six months later, he called again and rescheduled the training (Reconnected). I went. At that first event, people from other denominations were present, including those from The Salvation Army. They invited me back to train for them in their training colleges in both Brisbane and Sydney.
- Those connections have lasted over twenty years. And at the time of the writing of this book, I am invited back again for my nineteenth trip to Australia. All as a result of a single connection at a training event in Hershey.
- If the pastor's wife had not asked her husband whom to invite to the convention, I would have missed one of the grandest experiences of my life—that of training thousands of Australians.

The timing was perfect, the connections were valid, and it all fell together. I strongly believe that God provides the connections, but we have to respond to them. If the pastor's wife had called and I had said no, the whole twenty-year sequence probably would not have happened.

You could name many of these sequences yourself. All the people whom God has sent into your life are correctly timed for you to respond and grow. That is why expanding your relationships with other people is important. You never know where God's Spirit will guide you or where God wants to use you.

The Shifting of Passions

A different dimension to the ability to be in mission for others is when you discover that the passion you used to have for certain persons has shifted to another individual or group. This is the *shift of passions*. It is a reorientation of your life, a new direction, with new dreams and a new focus. Often, but not always, the shift takes place as a result of desert time. Some people make radical shifts. A friend was working as an executive in a large business. He was making a six-figure salary and enjoying a lovely home. Within a year he had shifted from working in the business world to going back to seminary and becoming a pastor. I was his coach while he was in seminary. His story is dramatic in the shift of values, beliefs, and focus on working with people in the church.

Because of his experience of working with executives, he has a wonderful skill set in working with all kinds of people. He once loved his job in business; he did it for many years, but something inside began to change. His emotions changed because he began, during the desert, shifting time, to see another vision that drew him to it. I asked him if he was moving away from the old vision or moving toward the new one. He said, "Yes." Both were moving at the same time. I experienced this same process when I left parish ministry and became a consultant and trainer. God sometimes pushes us to consider a new ministry, but more often God leads us toward the new.

Putting It Together

When life events are thrust on us and send us screaming into the desert, we find a place where new life can be born, new dreams can be identified, and our lives are rekindled with hope and joy in finding the new place, the new way of being. While this is going on in us, God is eminently present, coaching us, beckoning to us, to become who we can be.

Sometimes music and Scripture come together to make our journey more meaningful. One Sunday our choir sang, using the words of Psalm 139.

> O LORD, you have searched me and known me.
> You know when I sit down and when I rise up;
> you discern my thoughts from far away.
> You search out my path and my lying down,
> and are acquainted with all my ways.
> Even before a word is on my tongue,
> O LORD, you know it completely. . . .
> If I take the wings of the morning
> and settle at the farthest limits of the sea,
> even there your hand shall lead me,
> and your right hand shall hold me fast.
> If I say, "Surely the darkness shall cover me,
> and the light around me become night,"
> even the darknes is not dark to you;
> the night is as bright as the day,
> for darkness is as light to you. . . .
> I praise you. (vv. 1-4, 9-14)[4]

In his marvelous book *Faith Is a Verb*, author Kenneth Stokes tells of the desire that people who have similar experiences feel to get together to share their common feelings and thoughts. I remember walking across the Syracuse University campus while working on my masters degree in education and noticing that a small group of students were gathered together—some holding portable radios and listening together. I walked up to the group when one of the people announced to me that John Kennedy had just been shot. We stayed a long time talking, some, in tears, holding onto one another.

Just remember those times when thousands of people are affected by an event: for example, the destruction of the shuttle *Challenger*, the collapse of the World Trade Center's twin towers in New York City, the tsunami in the south Pacific, the inauguration of President Barack Obama. These are times when many people of every nation, every creed, every style of life are united in common experience.

Now, I bring a challenge to you. Can you imagine what would happen if you brought together all the people in your church who had a strong passion for something in their lives? A Passion Conference, so to speak, where the energy of the group could stimulate and support the passion of many people. It would not have to be a big group, but one where each could share—in depth—the passions that give each person life and hope. You would discover the huge variety of God-given passions. Make it *A Celebration of Passions*. Let me know if you do it. I would love to know the results. You can contact me at jsavage2@insight.rr.com.

This chapter has been devoted to having you explore your passion for others. Reflecting on what you have read, can you identify people in your life who have a passion for others, for whom helping others is their mission? Is this one of your passions? Who can help you? How can you help, encourage, or inspire others to help them succeed?

What is your energy level, the energy level of your family, your congregation? Does it reflect a passion for the spiritual life of others? Do you have a passion for developing deep spirituality in others? Or do you have a passion for those who are poor, young, disabled, mentally ill, sick, elderly, foreign? What might it take for a congregation or faith community to develop more passion for others and for specific ministries or missions? In a moment, put the book down and reflect on these things. What does God want to communicate to you about this?

A Brief Summary

Christians with mature spiritual intelligence have five predictable characteristics. These qualities allow these persons to be congruent in their relationship with others and in their intimate relationship with God.

The regular use of these abilities and skills will help any Christian become more spiritually intelligent. If the reader will take this book seriously, and create a personal spiritual development plan, he or she can quickly increase his or her spiritual IQ.

So once more, here are the tasks for the reader's work and development. If the reader gets to know them well, they will serve the reader well.

1. The skill and ability to state what you believe about God, others, and yourself. To share with another what has happened to you in your own personal journey—the ability to be a witness.
2. The ability to communicate with God, which includes prayer as a form of dialogue.
3. The desire to simplify one's life through the disciplines of meditation, reflection, and contemplation.
4. The willingness to be stripped down inside so that internal struggles and challenges of desert times can be used to build character and understanding.

5. The passion to be in mission for others and to share one's self with the world. This involves study of the Scriptures and other mental disciplines that keep one's brain alive, and thus which allows one to continue for the purpose of expanding understanding about God, others, and oneself. This passion helps one find meaning in all things and events, giving one the ability to restructure and reframe life's experiences.

To summarize, spiritually intelligent Christians are those who share their faith with other persons. They are persons who, through prayer, have an intimate relationship with God; they have disciplines of reflection and spend time in meditation; they can enter their deepest spiritual struggles; are in mission for others; they have committed themselves to the practice of lifelong learning about the Scriptures and other mental disciplines; and they have the ability to search diligently for meaning and purpose in all of life's experiences.

It has been a wonderful experience writing this book. I pray that it will in many ways motivate you to develop all the skills and passions needed to become the best Christian you can be. Working at these skills will bring you closer to God/Christ, and therefore bring you meaning and purpose. Remember: you are loved by God and there is nothing you can do to stop it.

If I can ever be of any help on your journey, please contact me by e-mail: jsavage2@insight.rr.com, or www.thekilgoregroup.com.

Blessings on your journey,
John S. Savage, DMin

Appendix

Tools to Develop a Personal Spiritual Development Plan

These materials are designed to help you form a personal spiritual development plan. The pages that follow provide a form for each of the spiritual intelligences. They can help you become intentional in creating goals and processes to enrich your spiritual life. Take your time in filling them out. Be practical, set benchmarks, and find someone to help hold you accountable, so that you may find success in your journey toward spiritual maturity.

Please feel free to reproduce these pages from the appendix.

Know Your Own Story: Be a Witness

Name		
Specific Spiritual Behavioral Competency		
Spiritual Developmental Objective #1		
Action Plan	What:	When:
	What:	When:
Coach	Who:	Frequency:
Allocation of time for 12 months	Item:	Hours:
	Item:	Hours:
	Item:	Hours:
Financial Investment	Personal cost of hours:	$
Books, Training, Retreats	External costs:	
	Total cost:	$
Notes		

Review Dates						

Pray Deeply: Dialogue with God

Name		
Specific Spiritual Behavioral Competency		
Spiritual Developmental Objective #1		
Action Plan	What:	When:
	What:	When:
Coach	Who:	Frequency:
Allocation of time for 12 months	Item:	Hours:
	Item:	Hours:
	Item:	Hours:
Financial Investment	Personal cost of hours:	$
Books, Training, Retreats	External costs:	
	Total cost:	$
Notes		

Review Dates						

Simplify Your Desires: Learn to Meditate, Reflect, and Contemplate

Name						
Specific Spiritual Behavioral Competency						
Spiritual Developmental Objective #1						
Action Plan	What:			When:		
	What:			When:		
Coach	Who:			Frequency:		
Allocation of time for 12 months	Item:			Hours:		
	Item:			Hours:		
	Item:			Hours:		
Financial Investment	Personal cost of hours:			$		
Books, Training, Retreats	External costs:					
	Total cost:			$		
Notes						
Review Dates						

Face Your Challenges:
Finding God in the Spiritual Desert Times

Name		
Specific Spiritual Behavioral Competency		
Spiritual Developmental Objective #1		
Action Plan	What:	When:
	What:	When:
Coach	Who:	Frequency:
Allocation of time for 12 months	Item:	Hours:
	Item:	Hours:
	Item:	Hours:
Financial Investment	Personal cost of hours:	$
Books, Training, Retreats	External costs:	
	Total cost:	$
Notes		

Review Dates						

Expand Your Understanding: Learn, Find Meaning in Your Life, and Be in Mission for Others

Name		
Specific Spiritual Behavioral Competency		
Spiritual Developmental Objective #1		
Action Plan	What:	When:
	What:	When:
Coach	Who:	Frequency:
Allocation of time for 12 months	Item:	Hours:
	Item:	Hours:
	Item:	Hours:
Financial Investment	Personal cost of hours:	$
Books, Training, Retreats	External costs:	
	Total cost:	$
Notes		

Review Dates						

Notes

Step I. Know Your Own Story

1. Patricia Cook, *Discovering Your Congregation and Its Community: A Model for Newly Appointed or Inquisitive Pastors* (August 18, 2008), 18–19.

2. Daniel Goleman, *Emotional Intelligence* (New York: Bantam, 1995), 43. I urge everyone who wants to become spiritually intelligent to read Goleman's book(s). The book mentioned here is powerful and extremely important for your understanding of emotions. Read appendix A, "What Is Emotion?" 289.

3. John Savage, *Listening and Caring Skills: A Guide for Groups and Leaders* (Nashville: Abingdon, 1996).

4. Joseph Chilton Pearce, *The Death of Religion and the Rebirth of Spirit* (Rochester, Vt.: Park Street, 2007).

5. Ron Willingham, *When Good Isn't Good Enough* (New York: Doubleday, 1988), 4–6.

6. Viktor E. Frankl, M.D., *The Doctor and the Soul: From Psychotherapy to Logotherapy* (New York: Vintage, 1986), 96–97.

Step II. Pray Deeply

1. Brother Lawrence, *The Practice of the Presence of God* (Worcester, Mass.: New Seeds Books, 2005), 22.

2. Ibid., vii.

3. *Diagnostic and Statistical Manual of Mental Disorders,* 4th ed. (Washington, D.C.: American Psychiatric Association, 1995), 147.

Step III. Simplify Your Desires

1. Elizabeth Barrett Browning, *Aurora Leigh*, Book VII. 821–22.

2. Georgia Harkness, *Prayer and the Common Life* (New York: Abingdon-Cokesbury, 1948), 135–36.

3. "If This Is Not a Place," music and lyrics by Ken Medema (copyright Word Music, LLC).

4. Steve Pavlina, *Personal Development for Smart People: The Conscious Pursuit of Personal Growth* (Carlsbad, Calif.: Hay House, 2008), 25.

5. Steve Pavlina, "Journaling," July 9, 2007. http://www.stevepavlina.com/blog/2007/07/journaling/ (accessed August 12, 2009).

6. Philip St. Romain, "Apophatic Meditation Methods," http://shalomplace.com/inetmin/contemplative/apophatic.html (accessed August 12, 2009).

Step IV. Face Your Challenges

1. Brother Roger of Taizé, "Letter from the Desert," *Rivers in the Desert,* ed. Rowland Croucher (Sydney, Australia: Albatross Books, 1991), 226.

2. Betty Stevens, "Thank You, Lord," *Rivers in the Desert,* ed. Rowland Croucher (Sydney, Australia: Albatross Books, 1991), 237.

3. Henri J. M. Nouwen, *The Way of the Heart: Desert Spirituality and Contemporary Ministry* (New York: Ballantine, 1985), 14–15.

4. Thomas R. Kelly, *A Testament of Devotion* (New York: Harper and Bros., 1941), 53.

Step V. Expand Your Understanding

1. This pattern represents the advanced and user-friendly "The Day End Review: An Advanced New Behavior Generator" as designed by Alexander Van Buren in *Anchor Point* 11, no. 11 (November 1997):22. While the original form was created by Alexander Van Buren, I have modified it for the purpose of spiritual reflection.

2. I have since taken even more advanced programs from the Posit Science organization. I am now participating in their beta test program.

3. Kilian McDonnell, "Marcia from Poland," in *Swift, Lord, You Are Not* (Collegeville, Minn.: Saint John's University Press, 2003), 89.

4. Our choir used an adaptation of this psalm that was set to music by Ben Harlan, which can be found at his website, www.benjaminharlan.com.

Bibliography

Chadwick, Harold J. *Brother Lawrence, The Practice of the Presence of God*. Alachua, Fla.: Bridge-Logos Publishers, 1999.

Frankl, Viktor E. *Man's Search for Meaning*. Boston: Beacon Press, 2006.

Goleman, Daniel. *Emotional Intelligence*. New York: Bantam Books, 1998.

Nouwen, Henri J. M. *Reaching Out—The Three Movements of the Spiritual Life*. Garden City, N.Y.: Doubleday, 1975.

Pearce, Joseph Chilton. *The Biology of Transcendence*. South Paris, Me.: Park Street Press, 2002.

Rediehs, Glen, and Larry E. Webb. *Healthy Church DNA*, Bloomington, Ind.: iUniverse, 2002.

Rosenthal, Norman E. *The Emotional Revolution*. New York: Kensington, 2002.

Savage, John S. *Listening and Caring Skills*. Nashville: Abingdon Press, 1996. (See especially "Story Listening," "Life Commandments," and "Story Polarization Listening.")

Stokes, Kenneth. *Faith Is a Verb—Dynamics of Adult Faith Development.* New London, Conn: Twenty-Third Publications, 1989.

Whitney, Donald S. *Spiritual Disciplines for the Christian Life.* Pueblo, Colo.: Navpress, 1991.

Zohar, Danah, and Dr. Ian Marshall. *Connecting with Our Spiritual Intelligence.* London, England: Bloomsbury, 2000.